According to the official development ideology of the 1990s, political reform must accompany economic liberalization. Investors, lenders, and aid donors have become disillusioned with autocrats who are unable to foster private investment and economic recovery. Reinforcing the reformist trend are the demise of the Cold War and widespread popular protests against authoritarian regimes in the non-Western world. A revised official consensus has thus emerged: African recovery requires not only a reduction in the size and economic role of monopolistic and inefficient states, but also their transformation into capable and accountable liberal democracies.

Is this a desirable and practicable political programme? Certainly democratic experiments have begun all over Africa. The number of liberal democracies is growing, and many multi-party elections are promised in the near future. But can liberal democracies survive and are they conducive to renewed economic growth?

Richard Sandbrook answers these questions, and assesses the feasibility of the new political programme in establishing Africa's economic recovery. He argues that the programme has merit as a short-term, emergency strategy but, in the longer term, a more self-reliant, state-directed approach should be adopted to ensure prosperity and durable democracy in the region.

AFRICAN SOCIETY TODAY

General editor: ROBIN COHEN

Advisory editors: O. Aribiah, Jean Copans,
Paul Lubeck, Philip M. Mbithi, M. S. Muntemba,
O. Nnoli, Richard Sandbrook

The series provides scholarly, but lively and up-to-date, books, which appeal to a wide readership. The authors are drawn from the field of development studies and all the social sciences, and have had experience of teaching and research in a number of African countries.

The books deal with the various social groups and classes that comprise contemporary African society, and the interlinked volumes create an integrated and comprehensive picture of the African social structure.

Also in the series

Farm labour. KEN SWINDELL

Migrant laborers. SHARON STICHTER

The politics of Africa's economic stagnation. RICHARD SANDBROOK

Inequality in Africa: political elites, proletariat, peasants and the poor.
E. WAYNE NAFZIGER

The African worker. BILL FREUND

African capitalism. PAUL KENNEDY

Rural society under stress. JONATHAN BARKER

THE POLITICS OF AFRICA'S ECONOMIC RECOVERY

RICHARD SANDBROOK

Professor of Political Science
University of Toronto

CAMBRIDGE
UNIVERSITY PRESS

Published by the Press Syndicate of the University of Cambridge
The Pitt Building, Trumpington Street, Cambridge CB2 1RP
40 West 20th Street, New York, NY 10011–4211, USA
10 Stamford Road, Oakleigh, Victoria 3166, Australia

First published 1993

Printed in Great Britain by Redwood Press Limited,
Melksham, Wiltshire

A catalogue record for this book is available from the British Library

Library of Congress cataloguing in publication data
Sandbrook, Richard.
The politics of Africa's economic recovery/Richard Sandbrook.
p.   cm. – (African society today)
Includes bibliographical references and index.
ISBN 0 521 41543 8 (hc). – ISBN 0521 42563 8 (pb)
1. Africa –Politics and government – 1960–   2. Africa – Economic
conditions – 1960–   3. Democracy – Africa.   I. Title.   II. Series.
JQ1879.A15S26 1993
960.3'29 – dc20   92–10888 CIP

ISBN 0 521 41543 8 hardback
ISBN 0 521 42563 8 paperback

To R. Cranford Pratt, teacher, colleague, friend

Life springs from ultimate resignation. Uncomplaining acceptance of the reality of society gives man indomitable courage and strength to remove all removable injustice and unfreedom.
Karl Polanyi, *The Great Transformation*

CONTENTS

TABLES

ACKNOWLEDGEMENTS

I wish to acknowledge the considerable assistance I have received in preparing this study. The Social Sciences and Humanities Research Council of Canada provided a generous two-year research grant (1989–91). The Montreal-based International Centre for Human Rights and Democratic Development funded an Empowerment Project in 1990–2 which helped me to clarify the ideas developed here. One phase of the project involved a conference in Arusha, Tanzania, in August 1991 on 'Empowering People: Civil Associations and Democratic Development in Sub-Saharan Africa'. I learned a great deal about the tribulations and strategies of social movements and nongovernmental organizations from the activists from eight African countries who attended. A grant from the Canadian International Development Agency allowed me to travel extensively in Africa to make contacts in the groundwork for this conference. This was an invaluable part of my general education on democratic movements and economic recovery in Africa.

I received, as usual, much intellectual support from friends and colleagues. Dr Mohamed Halfani and Professor Eboe Hutchful, my co-organizers of the Arusha conference, brought stimulating and divergent perspectives to my attention. Professors Robin Cohen and Cranford Pratt offered cogent criticisms of an earlier version of this book. Marie Gottschalk, an Associate Editor of the *World Policy Journal*, prodded me to clarify my position in a summary article I wrote for the journal. And Judith Barker Sandbrook, as always, contributed sound editorial advice. I alone am responsible for any remaining errors.

Finally, I thank Fela Anikulapo-Kuti and Kalakuta Limited of Lagos for permission to quote several lines from the song 'Beast of No Nations'.

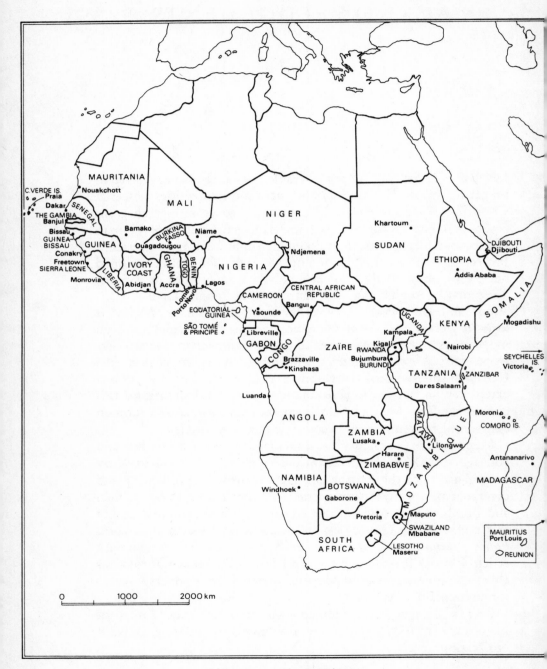

African states and principal cities

§ 1 §

THE REDISCOVERY OF POLITICS

'Worshipping a dictator,' as a fictional hero of Chinua Achebe so aptly proclaims, 'is such a pain in the ass'. 'It wouldn't be so bad,' this hero observes, 'if it was merely a matter of dancing upside down on your head. With practice anyone could learn to do that. The real problem is having no way of knowing from one day to another, from one minute to the next, just what is up and what is down' (Achebe 1987: 45). This conviction would have been shared by many Africans as the 1990s dawned. Political demonstrations and riots rocked most one-party states and military juntas between 1989 and 1991. People were fed up with erratic, self-serving, and corrupt – not to mention oppressive – governance.

This ferment coincided with a dramatic shift in the development establishment's view of what needed to be done to reverse sub-Saharan Africa's economic decline. On the one hand, the tarnished allure of socialism and the waning of the Cold War had eroded the Western powers' strategic interest in protecting friendly, yet manifestly unpopular, African dictators. On the other hand, many authoritarian African regimes had succumbed to a capricious and predatory economic management. The World Bank and International Monetary Fund (IMF) could attribute a decade of disappointing results from market-oriented structural adjustment primarily to this mismanagement, rather than to the inadequacies of their recommended policy reforms or the vagaries of the international economic order. Development agencies therefore found it both geopolitically and intellectually acceptable to contend that, in Africa as elsewhere, glasnost must accompany perestroika. Western governments, international organizations, and even some African governments rediscovered an enthusiasm for good government, to be achieved by political in addition to economic liberalization.

I

The World Bank has, as usual, played a central role in formulating the current development ideology. The Bank's seminal report of November 1989, *Sub-Saharan Africa: From Crisis to Sustainable Growth* (World Bank 1989a), is an exceptionally clear and authoritative account of the ascendent liberal-democratic, free-enterprise model for Africa's recovery. This model, like all development ideologies, identifies societal goals, which, besides growth, now encompass such laudable ends as ecological sustainability, equity (including gender equality), agricultural expansion, and democratization. It also furnishes a general explanatory framework which weighs the impediments to these goals (primarily growth) in the form of domestic versus international variables, and economic as opposed to political, social, and cultural factors. On this basis, the model proposes guidelines for efficacious policy and institutional reforms.

The current ideology is not really new. It is a revision of the orthodoxy prevailing in the 1980s, not an entirely different approach. In the 1950s and 1960s, the dominant development model assumed that markets often worked inefficiently in developing countries, and that therefore a pro-active state must widely intervene to counter these market failures. But, in the late 1970s and 1980s, disillusion with statist approaches and the ascendancy of neo-conservative governments in Britain, the United States, and West Germany provoked a shift toward a neo-classical, market-oriented paradigm. Development policy then focused on the role of markets, the price mechanism, and the private sector. Domestic failings in the form of mistaken policies, not the workings of the global economy, were identified as the prime cause of economic stagnation in the Third World. Today's revised development ideology retains both the emphasis upon domestic sources of economic malaise, and the faith in liberal economic policies. What is new is the belated recognition of the centrality of the state, and in particular, accountable government, to sustained capitalist development.

'Africa needs not just less government but better government – government that concentrates its efforts less on direct [economic] interventions and more on enabling others to be productive' (World Bank 1989a: 5). This distils the essence of the new development ideology's political message. A precondition of capitalist development is a state which is able and willing to safeguard political order and foster an adequate infrastructure, a calculable law and

administration, and consistent, market-facilitating economic policies. Yet what characterized most African countries, claimed the
Bank's report, was a bloated, overextended state of limited capacity
that was given to disorder, capricious management, and faulty
policy. Hence, the Leviathan must be tamed, redirected, and made
effective. How? The Bank proposed, in effect, to convert the monopolistic African states into liberal democracies linked to enlarged
and rejuvenated private sectors, and to rebuild the reformed states'
institutional capacity.

This programme commands wide official support today. Even
such a tenacious critic of World Bank policies as Dr Adebayo
Adedeji, the former Executive Secretary of the United Nations
Economic Commission for Africa (ECA), has accepted the 1989
report as 'an important contribution to building a consensus on the
vital policy issues that confront Africa' (Morna 1990: 53). This
consensus manifests itself in new political conditions attached to aid
and loans. Douglas Hurd, the British Secretary of State for Foreign
and Commonwealth Affairs, bluntly identified these conditions in a
speech in June 1990. Potential recipients of Western aid must, he
warned, be countries 'tending towards pluralism, public accountability, respect for the rule of law, human rights and market principles'. Governments which persist with 'repression, corrupt
management, or with wasteful and discredited economic policies
should not expect us to support their folly with scarce resources
which could be used better elsewhere' (*West Africa* 25 June–1 July
1990: 1077). Britain's European partners were in accord with such
political conditionality, judging by a new European Community
charter signed in November 1991. This charter linked aid to respect
for human rights, democratization, a free press, and probity in
aid-recipient countries. The United States government also enthusi-
astically endorsed the new consensus in 1990–1. Both the US State
Department and the US Agency for International Development
adopted programmes to promote good governance and democracy.
Japan, now the world's largest aid donor, has also fallen into line.

The Kenyan government of President Daniel arap Moi felt the full
force of the new policy in 1991. Kenya had long been a favoured
recipient of Western aid. Despite human-rights abuses, failures to
implement agreed economic reforms, and an increasingly anaemic
economic performance, Kenya had seen its grants rise from 1 per
cent of its GDP in 1986 to more than 3 per cent in 1990 (*The*

Financial Times, London: 8 Jan. 1992). Yet Kenya's aid donors, meeting in Paris under the World Bank's chairmanship in November 1991, announced an unprecedented six-month suspension of new aid pledges to Kenya. Moi's repressive responses to popular demands for multiparty democracy, combined with endemic corruption, maladministration, and growing official violence, precipitated this action. Within days, Moi reluctantly bowed to the pressure from internal dissenters and external aid donors; he lifted the ban on opposition parties and promised multiparty elections. The link between external aid and political as well as economic reform was firmly established.

But praise for the new strategy's support for democratic movements should not blind us to its broader ideological implications. It would be naive to treat the strategy's main proponents, the World Bank and the IMF, as non-ideological agencies open-endedly searching for cures for Africa's financial disequilibria, stagnation, poverty, and oppression. The geopolitical interests of the Western powers and (where these differ) the needs of internationalized capital will inevitably influence revisions in the dominant development ideology. Since their creation, the IMF and the World Bank have consistently aimed to integrate as many national economies as possible into a multilateral global capitalist economy (Wood 1986). Both agencies have encouraged, in countries receiving their loans, monetary, fiscal, and trade policies which extend the sway of international market forces. Open, export-oriented development may meet the needs of international capital and the advanced industrial countries; it does not necessarily advance the interests of the poor within low-income developing countries.

Scepticism is therefore warranted in posing the critical question: does the liberal-democratic, free-enterprise model constitute a plausible political programme for arresting Africa's downward spiral? Not, of course, that African governments have much choice in the matter. International financial institutions afford Africa 'the only game in town', in light of the paucity of private capital flows to Africa, the virtual demise of socialism, and the weakened capacity of African governments to resist external blandishments. But are there positive reasons for adopting the strategy?

I will argue that, despite contradictions and shortcomings, the model offers the best option in the short run of the 1990s. In the longer term, however, a more transformational approach is required to deal with Africa's complex crisis.

However one evaluates the revised development model, few would deny that a rethinking of conventional development strategy in 1989–90 was long overdue. Sub-Saharan Africa had suffered a protracted and calamitous economic crisis that conventional adjustment policies had stemmed only in rare cases.

As the United Nations Secretary-General warned in his 1991 report *Economic Crisis in Africa*, Africa is heading for 'an unrelenting crisis of tragic proportions'. In the 1980s the sub-continent suffered a precipitous fall in per capita incomes from levels that were already intolerably low. Whereas per-capita incomes increased at a moderate rate of 1.4 per cent in the 1960s, this rate declined to 0.2 per cent in the 1970s and − 2.8 per cent between 1980 and 1986. Consequently, the number of Africans enduring absolute poverty grew by almost two-thirds in the first half of the 1980s to constitute more than half of the population; in the developing world as a whole the number rose by only a fifth. People in many African countries, for example Nigeria, Liberia and Niger, have endured a decline in real incomes of well over 25 per cent. Even under the sanguine assumption that the region achieves an annual growth rate of 4 per cent in the 1990s, sub-Saharan Africa will still suffer an increase of 85 million in the numbers of the poor by the year 2000. Whereas Asia's share of the world's absolute poor would decline from 72 to 53 per cent, Africa's would double from 16 to 32 per cent (World Bank 1990a; UNDP 1990).

Unfortunately, Africa's decline is not limited to a single sector. Per capita agricultural output has stagnated or declined. Industrial output has fallen. Deforestation and desertification have reduced the productive land area. Rising food imports, declining terms of trade, and capital flight have produced a massive jump in the external debt, which in 1990 was roughly equivalent to the sub-Saharan countries' gross national product and required half of all export earnings to service. Institutions, including once-proud universities, have decayed as budgets declined and patronage appointments vitiated managerial effectiveness.

Drastic reductions in social expenditures since 1980 have made everyday life for many a constant struggle. In the 1960s and 1970s, basic health indicators, including life expectancy and infant mortality rates, improved markedly. During this period, school enrolments grew faster than in any other region, with the primary school population nearly doubling. But budgetary cutbacks and declining incomes in the 1980s devastated many educational institutions, raised infant mortality rates, and worsened nutritional levels. Literacy rates, life expectancy, and employment in the formal economy remained stagnant or even declined.

However, the record is far from uniformly bleak in the forty-seven countries lying in or off the coast of sub-Saharan Africa. Botswana, Cameroon, Lesotho, and Mauritius have been consistently high economic performers, and Côte d'Ivoire, Gabon, Kenya, Malawi, Mali, Niger, Senegal, Tanzania, and Zimbabwe have experienced either high growth in the early years or modest growth throughout most of the period since independence. And some of the poorer countries, such as Tanzania, rank higher on the human development scale than many other countries with higher per capita Gross National Products (UNDP 1990: 128). Nonetheless, most Africans in 1991 were as poor or poorer than at independence three decades earlier.

Of course, there are striking contrasts. Whereas downtown Harare, Zimbabwe and Gaborone, Botswana boast neat, well-tended streets and buildings, orderly traffic flows, well-stocked stores, and an air of prosperity (despite the beggars and street children), other capitals, such as Freetown, Sierra Leone or Lagos, Nigeria resemble overgrown and overcrowded shanty-towns replete with crumbling buildings, open drains, and eroded and chaotic roads. It is no wonder that new regional headquarters of intergovernmental and non-governmental organizations proliferate in Harare as they once did in Nairobi and Accra.

Sierra Leone, a West African country of only 4 million, demonstrates what human devastation economic decline can bring. Once, between 1950 and 1972, the country had one of the fastest growing economies in the region (with an average annual growth rate of about 7 per cent). Although Sierra Leone is small in population, it is rich in minerals – diamonds, gold, bauxite, rutile, iron ore, chrome, and platinum. It also possesses relatively fertile land, together with abundant rainfall. Its shores teem with fish. And, during the colonial period, the territory developed a sound educational system, including a renowned university college. But the country entered a severe and unending economic crisis in the late 1970s. Incomes per capita declined by an average 5.6 per cent per annum in 1980–5. Inflation reached 80 per cent by the end of the decade. Pauperization was the consequence for professionals such as teachers and bureaucrats as well as for workers and others. Salary and wage-earners had no choice but recourse to informal economic activities in order to supplement their meagre family incomes. In Sierra Leone, as an observer notes (Zack-Williams 1991: 9), 'everyone trades: from little children who sell kerosene and fruits ... to women who sell cooked food to the urban poor; or politicians who use their influence to obtain import licences and set themselves or relations up in trading activities'. As well, teachers often moonlight as private tutors. Households with cars (or access to an employer's car) utilize them as taxis.

Meanwhile, the public services decayed (Zack-Williams 1990: 26–8). State hospitals and clinics went into a steep decline in the 1980s. Employees in these institutions suffered the same fate as teachers and other civil servants – shrinking real wages and non-payment of salaries for months on end. The resulting demoralization has negatively affected health services. Corrupt officials made matters worse by illegally diverting drugs and medical equipment to private clinics and drug stores. Private clinics have flourished; however, only members of the political and economic elite can afford their high prices. It is not surprising that the country now has a relatively poor health record. Life expectancy is only 42 years; 170 of every 1,000 children die before age 1; and 43 of every 1,000 children between the ages of 1 and 4 die each year (World Bank 1988c: 214).

Education is in equally dire straits. Many schools are so dilapidated that they lack windows and roofs, as well as supplies (Zack-Williams 1990: 28). The expense of keeping children in school means that almost half of the eligible children do not attend primary school. Even those who do attend receive an education of inferior quality to that of the 1970s, owing to overcrowded classrooms, demoralized teachers, and a paucity of supplies and books. Even the renowned colleges of Freetown have declined to mere shadows of their former glory. Falling academic salaries and deteriorating conditions produced an exodus of qualified faculty, either to positions abroad or to lucrative consultancies for foreign organizations. Adult illiteracy stands at 71 per cent, and only 21 per cent of women are literate.

The road system in Sierra Leone also fell apart in the 1980s. Roads, even in the towns and cities, were so dilapidated by 1989 that the official car of choice for cabinet ministers, senior civil servants, and judges was a rugged Japanese jeep (Zack-Williams 1990: 28).

Life was equally hard elsewhere. In Ghana, reputedly a success story of structural adjustment, the new minimum daily wage of 170 cedis in 1989 barely paid for a can of milk and represented only about half of the cost of a bar of laundry soap. Obviously, the households of urban workers could not survive without recourse to multiple job-holding and informal income opportunities. But even middle-class professionals were severely affected by the economic crisis. Witness the plight of Joe Mensah, a senior civil servant in Accra, Ghana (Morna 1989: 46–7). When he graduated from law school in 1972, he expected to be able to afford a car, a house, and modern appliances within a few years. He had not been able to buy a house by 1989, however, and a car he purchased in 1976 subsequently had to be sold to support his family of four. By 1989, Mensah earned a salary equivalent to $US50 per month. His wife earned $US30 per month. Their total formal incomes fell short of the $US100 per month needed to pay for their household's bare necessities. Mensah, not surprisingly, was unimpressed by six years of Economic Recovery Programmes: 'At a time when I should be sitting back and enjoying myself, I find myself even worse off than when I began' (Morna 1989: 47).

If it were not for the unenumerated and unregulated informal or parallel economy, life would be even more desperate than it is. Tanzania, in the midst of an economic recovery programme in 1989, brought in a higher scale of civil-service salaries; but the scale ranged only from $US10 to $64 per month at the official rate of exchange. True, fringe benefits such as housing allowances augmented salaries. Nonetheless, a sack of maize (the country's staple food) cost over $US7.50; public secondary school fees ranged from $US11 to $22 a year; income taxes, exclusive of other levies, removed $US3.50 from a monthly salary of $US30; and rents rose markedly (Spear 1989: 46). Virtually all Tanzanian civil servants thus had to supplement their earnings, usually in the parallel economy. Farming and animal husbandry are common sidelines. Even professionals have small farms on which they produce milk, eggs, and chickens for urban markets. Such activities allow families to double or treble their incomes (Spear 1989: 46). Whereas an average school teacher earned $US30 per month in 1989, a cow could fetch $US60. Other enterprising civil servants (or even those with farms) made money by converting the front room of their houses to a shop; using their family car as a taxi; establishing back-lane workshops to make furniture or repair automobiles; or engaging in black-market activities such as currency deals. Most of these activities escaped taxation.

Informal economic activities are widespread in all countries, as people find ingenious if not always legal ways to survive. In extreme cases of economic decline, such as Zaire and Uganda, the underground economy has accounted for as much as two-thirds of Gross Domestic Product (Schissel 1989: 43). Petty commercial and productive activities, similar to those described in the cases of Sierra Leone and Tanzania, comprise a large part of the parallel economy in most countries. Finance constitutes another dynamic informal activity in countries whose banks are unreliable as a source of credit. In Cameroon, for instance, *tontines* (informal credit associations) are a major source of credit to those who lack collateral. These associations are reputed to handle more money than official banks, and, though unofficial, rarely suffer from defaults (Schissel 1989: 45). International trade, or smuggling, is another major dimension of the underground economy. Traders ignore international boundaries as they move goods and money from place to place. For instance, Nigerian traders smuggle locally manufactured goods to Cameroon where they are sold for CFA francs. They then trade these francs in Lomé, Togo, for hard currencies receivable in European centres. Agents use these funds to buy products which are then smuggled, via Lomé, into Nigeria. The circle is then complete (Schissel 1989: 45).

To rejuvenate slumping economies, the World Bank and International Monetary Fund have sponsored structural adjustment programmes which, in effect, encourage the state-dominated 'first' (formal) economy to emulate the competitive 'second' (informal) economy.[1] The bulk of sub-Saharan countries have attempted at least one such programme since 1980. A typical structural adjustment programme of the World Bank included measures to maximize reliance upon markets in goods, capital, and labour flows; to minimize governmental expenditures and economic interventions by reducing public ownership, subsidies, price controls, and regulation; and to improve the state's efficiency in allocating and using resources. In implementing such programmes, the Bank and the IMF in the 1980s eschewed consideration of the political constraints and concerns of the recipient countries, except insofar as these obstructed a government's ability to impose technically 'correct' economic policies.

The efficacy of these programmes was a subject of heated debate in the 1980s. Disputes raged owing to the ambiguity of structural adjustment – no one could say what would have happened to a particular economy in the absence of 'economic reform' – and disagreements over the criteria of evaluation. Proponents tended to focus on aggregate economic indicators, such as Gross Domestic Product, agricultural output, exports, fiscal balances, and inflation. Opponents questioned the social costs of adjustment, its contribution to long-term growth and development, and the external indebtedness and dependency that resulted.

Ghana's experience demonstrates the difficulty of reaching a conclusive judgement. Often touted as a 'success story', it was in the midst of its third Economic Recovery Programme in 1991. In 1983, when the radical populist government of Flight-Lieutenant Jerry Rawlings shifted course to embrace IMF-sponsored structural adjustment, the economy was widely regarded as a basket-case (Harsch 1989: 23). Between 1970 and 1982, Ghana's gross domestic product had declined at an average annual rate of 0.5 per cent. This amounted to a fall in real per capita income of nearly a third. Inflation had reached 123 per cent in 1983. The infant mortality rate had risen from 80 per 1,000 in 1975 to 107 per 1,000 in 1983. As a result of official price controls, most economic activity had shifted to the parallel economy. The public sector was saddled with tens of thousands of redundant employees. Corruption pervaded the system.

Structural adjustment policies registered considerable improvements in some economic indicators between 1984 and 1989 (Loxley 1991). Annual economic growth rose into the 5–6 per cent range – which translated into a per capita growth rate of 2½–3 per cent per annum, at a time when per capita growth rates elsewhere in the region were usually negative. Food production per capita grew. The manufacturing sector expanded. The rate of investment increased, albeit slowly. Although exports failed to meet targets, this flowed from the fall of 54 per cent in the world price of cocoa between 1986 and 1990. (The volume of cocoa exports rose by a third as export receipts fell.) Nonetheless, external debt mushroomed as aid and loans were used to finance almost half of Ghana's imports. Between 1983 and 1988, the foreign debt had more than doubled, to $US3.3

billion. The government managed to balance its budget – until 1990. And inflation fell from its peak of 123 per cent in 1983 to about 40 per cent in 1990 (which was higher than in 1989 owing to disastrous export sales and poor weather).

Although this is an impressive record, dissenters point to various problems and shortcomings. Ghana is as dependent as ever upon the export of cocoa, whose world price has collapsed. Inflation is on the increase again. Contrary to the expectations of the IMF and Rawlings government, foreign investors have shown no interest in Ghana despite its extensive economic restructuring. The enormous debt load will constrain further growth. Many Ghanaians seem not to have benefited from the improvement in aggregate economic indicators. And, they say, the replicability of the Ghanaian experience in Africa is dubious, owing to the unwillingness of Western governments and the international financial institutions to commit elsewhere the same level of resources which they have directed to Ghana.

In light of the controversies surrounding the evaluation of structural adjustment even in the dramatic case of Ghana, prudence dictates a circumspect judgement. Structural adjustment programmes had mixed but often disappointing results in sub-Saharan Africa in the 1980s. The international financial institutions have tried to put the best face on the adjustment record. A report issued by the World Bank and United Nations Development Program in early 1989 concluded that 'evidence suggests that reforms and adjustment generally have led to better economic performance in the region' (World Bank 1989b: 27). But the Economic Commission for Africa and independent scholars have cogently challenged this report, including its methodology (United Nations Economic Commission for Africa 1989; Helleiner 1990: 9–10; Ravenhill 1990: 708–9). A 1988 'Mid-Term Review' by the UN's Program of Action for African Economic Recovery and Development reached a conclusion on structural adjustment that more accurately reflects the evidence and independent evaluations: 'a handful of countries registered some improvement in their overall economic fortunes. For a slightly greater number, there have been positive trends in certain macroeconomic indicators (higher export volumes, lower inflation rates, reduced budgetary deficits). But for a majority of African states, there has not been even a hint of recovery.'[2]

Development models should generate useful advice to deal with these pressing socio-economic problems. Prescriptions are likely to be only as good as the explanatory framework from which they are deduced. The political-economic perspective of the current development ideology is an improvement on the narrowly technocratic one it replaced. Yet both the current model and its predecessor have underestimated the role of global constraints on Africa's recovery. Most of the responsibility for Africa's crisis is still pinned on domestic failings.

A useful model must capture the complex interconnection of political and economic, domestic and international, factors in economic decline. A brief reference to Togolese experience may starkly illustrate these interconnections. Togo, a 'least-developed' West African country of 3.5 million, has long been heavily dependent upon the export of phosphate. When the world price for phosphate escalated in the mid-1970s, the government of the autocratic president, Gnassingbe Eyedéma, decided to use its foreign exchange bonanza to finance import-substitution industries behind high tariff walls. The result was a disaster:

Attracted by the new wealth, many European entrepreneurs and crooks appeared on the scene. Corruptibility and the robber baron mentality complemented each other. But before long the price of phosphate collapsed. Togo's foreign debt exploded and reached one billion dollars. Since 1979, one debt rescheduling has followed another. The profiteers of that time have long since been home free with their loot, thanks to state guarantees of their own countries.... The private creditors have thus been replaced by states who extract interest and loan repayments from Togo. In Togo, those circles that raked in exorbitant sums of corruption money and were responsible for the wrong decisions taken are hardly the ones suffering from the debt burden. It is the population at large and the farmers [who] pay for the failed industrialization. (Gerster 1989: 26)

With a foreign debt equal to its national income, Togo was one of the first African countries to undertake a structural adjustment programme, in 1979. In 1991 the country was in the midst of its fourth such programme. Eyedéma in the 1980s became a favourite of the World Bank and the IMF because of his enthusiasm for market solutions and his apparent popularity.

But, in 1990, the myth was shattered. In October, only four months after the government had organized an anti-multiparty demonstration of 50,000 people, the security forces battled rioters in

Lomé leaving 17 dead and 170 in detention. The riots followed a brutal police action against demonstrators denouncing alleged kangaroo-court convictions of two political dissidents. Following a further week of demonstrations and riots in Lomé in March 1991, Eyedéma surrendered to the demands of the democratic opposition. He promised to move to a multiparty electoral system. However, by the end of 1991, Eyedéma was still using his personal control of elite forces in the army to frustrate his democratic opposition, organized into a 'national conference', and to manage an increasingly questionable transition to democracy.

Togo's experience demonstrates the perils of both an outward-oriented economic strategy and an unaccountable and self-serving regime. All the ingredients are present: oscillating world prices for the principal commodity export; foreign corporations eager for quick profits so long as their loans and investments are guaranteed; corrupt political insiders and civil servants; and an authoritarian government able to keep the lid on internal dissent (until 1990–1) and gain the backing of the international financial institutions. And, as usual, ordinary citizens, including the middle classes, foot the bill for the wrongheaded policies, mismanagement, and collusive deals.

To what extent can the development ideologies of the 1980s and 1990s account for the complex array of factors that brought the Togolese economy to its knees?

Accelerated Development in Sub-Saharan Africa, a report issued by the World Bank in 1981, shaped donors' thinking about development strategy in the 1980s as much as *Sub-Saharan Africa: From Crisis to Sustainable Growth* is doing in the 1990s. The Berg report (as the 1981 report is often called) recognized some internal 'structural' constraints upon growth – such as underdeveloped human resources, hostile climatic and geographic factors, and an unprecedented rate of population growth. It also acknowledged some external constraints in the form of such adverse trends in the international economy as stagflation in the industrialized North, high energy prices, the slow growth of demand in Africa's primary commodities, and, for several commodities, adverse terms of trade. However, having listed these impediments, the report pinpointed 'domestic policy deficiencies' and 'administrative constraints' as the chief culprit blocking economic progress by retarding market efficiency (World Bank 1981: 4.1).

On the basis of this analysis, the Berg report recommended a range of policy reforms to facilitate largely unregulated market economies. It aimed, in particular, to remove the policy bias against agriculture by means of reform in price, tax, exchange-rate, and state marketing policies. The report hoped to stimulate agricultural output and exports in this way, in the well-founded expectation that agricultural growth in predominantly agrarian societies would accelerate overall development. The report also recommended that the size and economic responsibilities of African states be pruned, and that their capacity to formulate economic policy, manage essential public services, and vet development projects be upgraded.

The report was controversial in its day. It devoted too little attention to the myriad ways in which the international economy limited Africa's economic prospects. It assumed that Africa's future prosperity lay in its closer integration into the global economy, though the flat world demand for Africa's primary commodities, the ability of other regions to capture shares of already meagre world markets, and the propensity of manufacturers to develop substitutes for Africa's inputs made this a dubious proposition. Equally dubious was the view that interventionist states are necessarily inimical to economic development. However, the most striking weakness from the viewpoint of the World Bank's 1989(a) report is the Berg report's lack of a political context. It understood that administrative weaknesses impeded growth, but it did not trace these weaknesses to their political roots. For instance, the Berg report had little to say about the deleterious impact on economic decision-making of authoritarian one-party or military regimes, such as that in Togo. Yet clientelism, personalistic rule, lack of governmental accountability, and in many countries, political instability and internal wars, constituted major hindrances to accelerated development.

The current development ideology, though still de-emphasizing external constraints on Africa's development, does belatedly recognize real domestic political weaknesses that bedevil recovery. And the latter weaknesses, unlike the external factors, are in principle susceptible to reform by Africans – though often not without enormous struggle and sacrifice.

'Although many African countries have seen their development efforts disrupted by sharp falls in the world price of key commodities, viewed over the long term, falling per capita incomes for Africa as a whole since the late 1970s are explained largely by the declining level and efficiency of investment, compounded by accelerating population growth – and not primarily by external factors' (World Bank 1989a: 3). The passage neatly summarizes the relative significance attached to international factors in the official consensus.[3] It seems to understate their significance. For instance, sub-Saharan Africa's overdependence on a few commodity exports is the root of many problems. Primary commodities account for more than 90 per cent of the entire continent's exports, and over 70 per cent of these exports are unprocessed. Cocoa and coffee alone account for 40 per cent of the continent's agricultural exports. It is common for one or two commodities to dominate a country's export receipts. For instance, oil accounts for about 90 per cent of Nigeria's exports, uranium about 80 per cent of Niger's exports, bauxite (including aluminium) almost 80 per cent of Guinea's exports, and copper almost 60 per cent of Zaire's exports (*West Africa* 21–7 August 1989: 1360–1). Since 1986, Africa's average real commodity prices have been at their lowest ebb for several decades.

Consider what the decline in cocoa prices since 1986 has meant for Côte d'Ivoire, which depends heavily upon the export of cocoa and coffee. For two years, the government resisted the advice of the World Bank and the IMF to lower the producer prices for these crops in order to reflect the downward trend in world prices. However, the government's massive subsidy to growers could not be sustained. Its foreign debt ran out of control. In the 1989 marketing season, it slashed producer prices by almost half. Farmers suffered immensely from the underpayments they received in 1988 and the reduced official prices in 1989. Nutrition and health standards declined; school attendance in villages fell sharply as parents could no longer afford tuition fees, books, and uniforms; farmers could not buy the insecticides and fertilizers that boost yields by 30 per cent; and young people fled to the cities in growing numbers to escape rural misery (*West Africa* 4–10 Dec. 1989: 2018–19). The government sought to deal with its declining revenues by reducing the salaries of civil servants, raising taxes, and cutting services; these actions ignited the disaffection of key urban constituencies in 1990, leading to a wave of strikes and demonstrations that forced the government to back down and legalize opposition parties.

Enormous foreign debts constitute a major obstacle to Africa's recovery. Although the Bank's report acknowledges this external constraint too, much more is needed in the way of a concerted programme to mobilize Western official support behind a plausible remedy. Recovery will remain problematical (despite domestic reforms) as long as African governments devote a quarter, a third, or even more of their limited export earnings to debt service. If the aid donors had continued to increase their level of assistance, the economic situation would not be as dire. But official aid, which had been growing at the annual rate of 4 per cent in the 1980s, appeared to be levelling off in the 1990s. Commercial loans also dried up, while capital flight from sub-Saharan countries continued. And ironically, the IMF even became a net recipient in its financial transactions with governments on the continent. Without debt relief and new inflows of capital, Africa, as the UN Secretary-General's 1991 report *Economic Crisis in Africa* cautions, will 'continue in stagnation and despair, with repercussions for the entire world'.

This UN report recommends an expansion of development assistance, the cancellation of $US104 billion in official bilateral debt and semi-official export credits, and a substantial write-down of the $US23 billion of commercial debt and $US44 billion in debts to the IMF and World Bank. However, the chances of such major North–South resource transfers remain meagre.

While the prevailing development ideology underplays these international constraints, it cogently identifies significant domestic problems. Climatic shocks, desertification, and explosive population growth (all identified in the Bank's 1989 report), are intractable, long-term problems with high economic costs. For example, the continent's population will double, to 1 billion, between 1990 and 2010, unless stringent family planning programmes are instituted (or unless the AIDS epidemic continues unabated). If sluggish growth in agriculture and industry persists, this 3 per cent rate of population increase will guarantee stagnant or declining per capita incomes.

Of greatest significance are policy and governmental failings, according to the Bank's analysis. Inadequate governmental attention to the needs of agriculture, and the low level and declining efficiency of investment, are identified as major problems. An array of policy and budgetary reforms since the early 1980s have reduced the bias against agricultural producers in most countries. However, the second problem remains. Investors have been discouraged as incremental output generated by investment has dropped from 31 per cent of investment in the 1960s to 2.5 per cent in the 1980s

(World Bank 1989: 3). Governments, it is contended, bear a large responsibility for this inhospitable investment environment. In part, this environment derives from economic policies that distort market signals; conventional market-oriented reforms can allegedly correct these 'errors'. But the roots of the problem are now seen to lie deeper, in the institutional structure and practices of the state.

What legal, administrative, and political factors undermine the magnitude and efficiency of investment? The 1989 Bank report and speeches by IMF, World Bank, and Western government officials refer to all or some of the following. Bloated public administrations operate inefficiently, erratically and sometimes dishonestly, partly as a result of the many officials who are appointed and promoted on the basis of nepotistic, factional, and personal ties. Corruption creates administrative bottlenecks. The economic infrastructure deteriorates or operates irregularly. Breakdowns in the administration of justice and political instability foster uncertainty as to the sanctity of private property and contracts. Heavy-handed regulation of civil society by suspicious autocrats discourages autonomous, grassroots initiatives and provokes people to flee into the unregulated informal sector, into illegal activities like smuggling, or even into exile. Ambitious individuals seek to make their fortunes through parasitical manipulation of the government's regulatory and spending powers. Risk-taking entrepreneurial activities are seldom the quickest and easiest road to wealth. Manipulating state offices, contracts, regulations, licensed monopolies, access to foreign exchange and other underpriced goods and services is far more lucrative. We see, in the Bank's words, 'the appropriation of the machinery of government by the elite to serve their own interests' (World Bank 1989a: 192).

Perhaps all this represents merely a belated official recognition of the political preconditions of economic growth. It is hardly news to most Africans that a crisis of governance depresses growth by raising the costs of investment and lowering productivity. The question is: what can be done to rectify this crisis of governance? And what political reforms will promote liberty and equality, as well as growth?

The new official consensus proposes that mismanagement, governmental inefficiency, and political uncertainty be tackled by cutting back the size and role of the state, buttressing its capacities, and augmenting public accountability. In effect, a democratic politics is to be grafted onto a rejuvenated liberal state in the context of an increasingly competitive market society.

In declaring that 'Africa needs less government', the World Bank reaffirmed its abiding faith in the liberal state, one whose primary economic task is to maintain the conditions for private capital accumulation. The state is expected to assume 'a leading role in building human resources, administrative, and physical infrastructure capacity, while the goods-producing and noninfrastructure service sectors are left to the flexibility and incentives of private enterprise and market discipline' (World Bank 1989a: 186). The Bank thus continues to advocate privatization where possible, decentralization of services to the local level, and a lifting of bureaucratic controls.

Africa also needs better government, claimed the report. One aspect is the old nostrum of administrative reform. Hiring and promotion in the public service should be on the basis of merit, not political connections; civil servants must be properly trained and motivated to stay in their jobs and work conscientiously; managerial autonomy and clear guidelines and performance criteria must be accorded the remaining parastatals, and so on.

What is new is the emphasis the report – and the current development ideology – places on democratization. A disciplined, responsible, and responsive state is one which openly makes decisions, and one whose officials are publicly accountable for their actions. Public accountability requires a free press to monitor governmental performance and publicize abuses, the reinvigoration of local government, and the fostering of community participation and non-governmental organizations. The Bank casts itself as a champion of the masses in declaring that the goal should be 'to empower ordinary people to take charge of their lives, to make communities more responsible for their development, and to make governments listen to their people. Fostering a more pluralistic institutional structure – including nongovernmental organizations and stronger local government – is a means to these ends' (World Bank 1989a: 55). Although the Bank stops short of advocating a multiparty electoral system, in practice Western governments have equated democratization with such a system.

There is a degree of political calculation in the World Bank's advocacy of democracy and popular empowerment. With the re-democratization of Latin America and Eastern Europe and the political openings in East Asia, democracy is again in vogue. The Economic Commission for Africa, one of the Bank's severest critics, rhetorically embraced popular participation some time ago. Opening an ECA-sponsored International Conference on Popular Participation in the Recovery Process in Africa in 1990, the commission's executive director unequivocally declared that 'the democratization of the development process, by which we mean the empowerment of the people, their involvement in decision-making, in implementation and monitoring processes – is a *conditio sine qua non* for socio-economic recovery and transformation' (Adedeji 1990). The World Bank wants to move the ECA, the Organization of African Unity, and other institutional critics, onto its side, and adopting popular political themes is one means of doing so.

But sincerity aside, what matters is that powerful international bodies and governments have rhetorically embraced democratization and decentralization. This signals to oppressive regimes that they must now be wary of human-rights abuses, and to Africa's democratic opposition groups that they have enhanced leverage against authoritarian practices.

Yet, as succeeding chapters will show, the politics of liberal-democratic reform confront serious challenges. First, the Bank prescribes a minimal liberal state, but experience has shown – whether in nineteenth-century Russia or twentieth-century Japan, Taiwan, South Korea, and Singapore – that a pro-active interventionist government facilitates economic development. Secondly, the Bank and most other official agencies now recommend political liberalization and democracy, believing these will push Africa's states to become more responsible and less predatory. But the historical, socio-economic, and political conditions in much of Africa do not favour the establishment of durable democracies. Moreover, and this is the model's third flaw, democracy is no guarantee of what all sides say they are pursuing in Africa: equitable growth. Thus, radical alternative programmes to democratic capitalism, including socialism and people-centred development, are unlikely to fade away in Africa.

Nevertheless, despite its flaws, the liberal-democratic free-enterprise model has merit as a short-run strategy. Most African states had decayed and become predatory in the 1980s, as chapter 2 shows. It therefore makes sense – in the 1990s – to reduce the state's economic role, while devising ways to enhance governmental accountability and capabilities. Governments should be encouraged 'to manage less, but manage better' (World Bank 1991b: ix). Their partial disengagement from economic life will provide a breathing space in which to revitalize and reorient state apparatuses.

In the longer term, the ascendant development ideology is too limited to point the way to a prosperous twenty-first-century Africa. First, rapid development will require a larger and more pro-active governmental role than that envisaged in this model. Policy must aim to reconstruct a developmental state, able and willing to re-engage in the directive, yet market-facilitating, role that modern development requires. Secondly, the model's outwardly oriented, export-based strategy, though probably unavoidable in the 1990s, is inadequate in the longer run. It can succeed only under two conditions: high and sustained growth in the industrialized countries to create demand for Africa's exports; and an openness in these developed countries to imports from the South. However, the North's sluggish growth and protectionism of the early 1990s show no signs of abatement. A more self-reliant strategy, under the aegis of a reconstituted and democratized developmental state, may therefore constitute the brightest prospect for African prosperity.

§ 2 §

FALSE STARTS: CAPITALIST
AND SOCIALIST

'Underdevelopment can be conquered in twenty years', declared René Dumont in 1962 in a bluntly entitled book, *L'Afrique noire est mal partie* (Dumont 1966: 223). This didn't happen. By the mid-1980s, most Africans were as poor or poorer than they had been in 1962. Dumont's stirring, if naive, programme for a coordinated, North–South assault on African poverty never materialized.

Many promising African experiments faltered for reasons Dumont identified thirty years ago. The 'natural conditions' of Tropical Africa – soils, topography, climate – are indeed more severe than those in Europe and North America. The workings of the global market economy do not favour Africa's dependent, commodity-export economies. But, above all, '[m]en are responsible for the economic backwardness of Africa' – both Europeans who exploited the continent for many decades and Africans, especially those in government (Dumont 1966: 31). Dumont, in his forthright and iconoclastic fashion, was one of the first to condemn African governing elites for their selfishness, dishonesty, indifference to the needs of the wealth-creating peasantry, and adoption of colonial attitudes. They seemed intent, he concluded, in creating a 'modern version of Louis XV's court' (Dumont 1966: 65).

Dumont's political analysis, though impressionistic, was nevertheless prescient in recognizing an impending 'crisis of governance'. Without an elite committed to development, without incentives for productive rather than parasitical behaviour, and without a lean and efficient state bureaucracy, economic development, Dumont realized, would stall. And, it should be added, the more economically interventionist a state, the more deleterious will such political weaknesses be.

At independence, most African regimes favoured a balance

between market and state which placed heavy responsibilities upon the latter. An 'étatist' approach was more or less inevitable. Interventionist colonial traditions, the nationalist elite's visceral association of capitalism with imperialism, the weakness of an indigenous business class, a professed commitment to social equity, foreign expert advice, and the new state managers' drive for self-aggrandizement – all these historical factors pushed in a statist direction. The post-colonial regime therefore assumed not only the tasks of all modern states: protector of public order and property rights, provider of social and physical infrastructure, and macro-economic manager (i.e., manipulator of fiscal, monetary, and trade policies to promote growth and restrain inflation). It also appropriated the roles of economic regulator, planner, and, to varying degrees, entrepreneur. Where the government defined itself as socialist, the large-scale private sector might disappear altogether. Even in the capitalist cases, a plethora of public corporations usually emerged in the utilities, commercial, financial, transport, and industrial sectors.

Although a heavy reliance upon the state is not necessarily wrongheaded in early developmental stages, in practice African state-capitalist and socialist strategies have often failed. This failure is not only one of policy. More fundamentally, interventionist regimes cannot succeed (regardless of global economic factors) without the will to back productive rather than parasitical behaviour, and without the necessary extractive, political, and administrative capacities to support their responsibilities. African states have generally lacked both the will and the capacity.

Will is needed because growth depends both on the extraction of a surplus and its productive investment. The sacrifice that some endure through surplus extraction is justifiable only if that surplus is used to expand the wealth of their nation – and ultimately the well-being of those who suffer. The question is: does the power structure support the property and consumption rights of parasites or producers? And *which* parasites or producers?

The answers depend upon the outcomes of historically specific political struggles. If a hegemonic class or class coalition emerges, then the state reflects the long-term interests of this class or coalition. If the ascendant class is a bourgeoisie, then the state responds to the priorities of the capitalist relations of production. The ethos and power of an entrepreneurial class discipline the state. In principle, the hegemonic class may be the proletariat; then the state will protect collective property rights and socialized production. However, political struggles in many sub-Saharan countries have not yet yielded a class hegemony. In these cases, where the state wields considerable autonomy from class forces, the political will to reinforce productive economic activities must be generated *within* the state itself.

Patriotism and an acute external threat have occasionally substituted the self-discipline of a nationalist elite for the extrinsic discipline of a strong and vigilant civil society. But the cleavages, acute poverty, and recent history of African countries do not conduce to the formation of such a self-abnegating nationalist elite. Unfortunately, the socialist cases also fall victim to the poverty, divisions, and weakness of civil society, combined with externally supported insurrections. Socialist cadres are neither motivated and disciplined from below by an independently organized mass base, nor empowered by cohesiveness, self-discipline, and adequate resources to carry through a revolution from above.

The temptation, therefore, is for the state's executive to exercise its considerable autonomy from classes in defence of the interests of a parasitical coterie of political insiders. For instance, factionalized neo-patrimonial elites do not constitute an ascendant bourgeoisie: they have neither the will nor the independent power base to enforce productive priorities or discipline upon the state apparatus. Instead, they settle as individuals for the short-run advantages of state-assisted rent-seeking behaviour, even though this behaviour, by stifling efficiency and sustained growth, runs counter to the long-term interests of capital. Some elements of the emergent bourgeoisie, to be sure, demand economic and political reforms to facilitate capitalist development. However, for the powerful, the chance for easy short-run gains outweighs considerations of long-run growth.

States, whether nominally capitalist or socialist, have also lacked, irrespective of will, the necessary extractive, political, and administrative capacities. To act effectively, a regime must extract adequate resources from society, mobilize popular acceptance of its programmes, and employ a cohesive and competent bureaucracy which is insulated from day-to-day political demands. These capacities are mutually reinforcing. A state needs revenues to support its coercive and administrative apparatuses; and only the effective operation of an administration and a police force generates the needed resources.

But an efficient coercive and administrative apparatus is not a sufficient basis for a stable, calculable political order. Governments reliant on coercion are wholly dependent upon the means of repression, and thus vulnerable to a *coup d'état*. As well, they will have to contend with the debilitating effects of popular hostility or indifference: widespread tax evasion, passive disobedience, military recruits who are unwilling to fight, and eventually bureaucratic malaise and corruption. The effectiveness and efficiency of a government therefore fundamentally depends upon its political capacity – its ability to elicit willing compliance from its population.

Historical, social, and material conditions in Africa have impeded the development of states with the will and capacity to implement ambitious developmental programmes. This is a major reason why 'false starts' have plagued both capitalist and socialist tendencies. It is worth sketching these onerous conditions, before turning to a detailed examination of each of the principal challenges to state capacity-building.[1]

The indiscipline and limited capacities of most African states stem partly from their newness and origins in foreign conquest. In all but a handful of cases – Swaziland, Lesotho, Rwanda, Burundi, Ethiopia – the history of statehood began only with the imposition of colonial or semi-colonial rule towards the end of the nineteenth century. During the ensuring seventy or eighty years, the imperial powers transplanted institutional models from the metropolis within the arbitrarily drawn boundaries of their colonies. Before World War II, colonial governments were more or less adequate for their then limited tasks: the levying of taxes, the preservation of law and order, and the construction and maintenance of basic infrastructure and services. But the lack of any organic connections between recently installed governmental structures and the political traditions of their host societies, in addition to the often extreme cultural–linguistic diversity, would later impede state formation.

After independence, the new rulers tried to accumulate and centralize power on the basis of the inherited institutions. They aimed to neutralize opponents, usually regionally/ethnically based, and implement ambitious development programmes. But the limitations of state power soon became apparent.

Economic conditions, in particular the widespread poverty, hampered the consolidation of effective states. Poverty and the small populations of most of the new states constricted the fiscal basis of government. Even these inadequate revenues plunged in the downturn of the 1980s, tempting governments to print money and risk fuelling inflation. Most governments also had to operate with a paucity of skilled personnel. Educated manpower was in short supply at independence, thanks to the relative neglect of education by the colonial powers.[2] In 1960, only 31 per cent of school-age children were enrolled in primary schools in the former French colonies; the corresponding proportion of enrolled children in the Anglophone countries in the same year was 40 per cent, and in the former Belgian colonies, 50 per cent. Very few Africans had graduated from secondary schools or universities. Throughout the vast area of sub-Saharan Africa, there were perhaps 1,200 university graduates in 1960. Zaire, an extreme case, was reputed to have fewer than twenty university graduates at independence. To make matters worse, a drastic erosion of civil service salaries in the 1980s further depleted the ranks of highly qualified public employees, and demoralized those who remained.

Mass poverty, more fundamentally, fosters an invidious struggle for scarce resources that threatens bureaucratic elan or socialist commitment within the state apparatuses. Enrichment assumes a peculiar fascination in societies where many struggle simply to survive. A wealthy Ethiopian interviewee graphically explained this fascination to a reporter following the overthrow of Emperor Haile Selassie:

[D]o you know what money means in a poor country? ... In a rich country, money is a piece of paper with which you buy goods on the market. You are only a customer ... And in a poor country? In a poor country, money is a wonderful, thick hedge, dazzling and always blooming, which separates you from everything else. Through that hedge you do not see creeping poverty, you do not smell the stench of misery, and you do not hear the voices of the human dregs. But at the same time you know that all of that exists, and you feel proud because of your hedge. You have money; that means you have wings. You are the bird of paradise that everyone admires. (Kapuscinski 1983: 44–5)

Such an attitude clearly works against political rectitude and a disciplined state in low-income countries. Families regard employment in the public sector as the major, or perhaps the only, avenue for upward mobility. Politicians and civil servants thus come under enormous pressure from their kin and dependents for special favours; they risk censure if they resist such demands.

Social structural factors have also influenced political behaviour. The typical fluidity and fragmentation of class structures have hampered state-led efforts to promote either capitalist or collectivist development. Regimes' significant degree of autonomy from class forces has tempted state insiders to exploit the state for short-term advantage.

Classically, in capitalist development, the political ascendancy of business eventually ensures that capitalist priorities and requirements are also those of the state. The bourgeoisie's ascendancy derives from its economic power, from its ownership of assets in an economic sphere that is autonomous from the state. But, in Africa, both the limited scope of market relations outside the cities, and the politicization of the economic sphere, diminish the independent economic power of capital. The statist models of post-colonial development made economic success dependent upon political decisions. Hence, political power relations exercised through the state have conditioned property relations – in the modern or formal sector at least – as much or more than the reverse. In addition, the bourgeoisie is weakened by its limited numbers, its recent origins, and its fragmentation into foreign–local and ethnic/regional/communal fractions. These factors constrain the hegemonic pretensions of indigenous bourgeoisies, except in such thoroughly commercialized societies as Zimbabwe.[3]

The proletariat, whose struggles with capital and the state in Western societies have shaped the emergence of highly articulated social democracies, is in Africa minuscule, only partially separated from the means of production, and subject until recently to political repression. If anything, the power of the organized working class has declined during the economic crisis. This crisis, by shrinking the wage-earning force and compelling wage-workers to moonlight in self-employment, weakened proletarian identity and the cohesion of the labour movement. This is, of course, not universally true. Islands of proletarian identity and solidarity persist, especially in the traditional working-class strongholds in mines and the oil industry, on docks and railways, and in large factories. The Zambian copper miners, for example, have steadfastly pursued their collective interests and maintained their independence from the governing party since Zambia became a one-party state in 1973. In 1990, their union emerged as a locus of democratic demands, and as a leading element in the Movement for Multiparty Democracy.

In general, class structures are highly fluid in an era of rapid socio-economic change. The transition to a capitalist mode of production is still only partial. Most sub-Saharan countries comprise largely peasant societies. Besides capitalist production characterized by private property, wage labour, and production for the market, household self-provisioning and petty commodity production persist in town as well as country. To complicate matters, many economically active individuals 'straddle' class boundaries (see, e.g., Kitching 1980). It is still common for a male smallholder, for instance, to spend a considerable time in urban wage-employment. While he is so employed, he and other members of his household will earn extra income through self-employment in the parallel economy as artisans, traders, or urban farmers. A majority of citizens are thus part time or full time peasants, pastoralists, traders, artisans and casual labourers – groups whose limited capacity for class consciousness and action is widely acknowledged. This offers political elites an unusual leeway *vis-à-vis* domestic groups.

Political factors constitute a third set of influences on governmental crises. Most countries lack a long history of centralized rule or a homogeneous political tradition; this legacy denies the new rulers a firm foundation in the habitual compliance of the population. Once the solidarity forged in the anti-colonial struggle dissipated, it was difficult to reconstruct. The traditional legitimacy of precolonial polities was largely irrelevant in the culturally heterogeneous contemporary state. Patriotism was uncertain to elicit consent in countries where the newness of territorial units and the saliency of ethnicity vitiated a strong sense of national unity. And class ideologies that elsewhere have facilitated compliance, especially liberalism and socialism, have few roots to sustain them.

A 'natural', though not inevitable, tendency of rulers in these circumstances is to have recourse to patrimonial mechanisms of governance, to base their regimes on a coterie of regional and organizational notables (Sandbrook with Barker 1985). For Max Weber, patrimonialism was a form of authority that emerged in preindustrial societies with large and politically inert peasantries and a nobility which competed for the favour of the monarch (Weber 1947: 347–57). The politics of patrimonial rule was not ideologically based but directed only at the distribution of material resources, power, and prestige. It was a politics of factions, interrupted periodically by short-lived peasant rebellions and other disturbances.

But history does not repeat itself; the conditions of sub-Saharan Africa are only analogous to those of traditional patrimonialism. Neither wholly preindustrial societies nor hereditary monarchs and nobles are common here. And ideological themes and class conflicts do intrude. Nonetheless, before the democratic transitions beginning in 1990, many of Africa's peasant societies did feature 'presidential-monarchs', a *noblesse d'état* (not yet a bourgeoisie-for-itself), and a political life characterized predominantly by factional manoeuvring, clientelistic relations, and the exclusion of the peasantry. *Neo*-patrimonialism – a form of governance based chiefly upon personal loyalties, patron–client networks, and coercion – is still prevalent; democratization is unlikely to erase these ingrained traits of political life. Factional struggles will continue to be intense, as outcomes largely determine access to wealth as well as power and status in these societies of extreme scarcity:

Combats sans merci car ils se déroulent dans un double contexte de rareté materielle et de précarité politique. Quand le produit national but est bas et quand la conservation d'une position de pouvoir dépend de seule humeur du Prince, la tentation est grande d'exploiter au mieux et au plus vite 'la situation.' D'où le prédation débridée de la part des entrepreneurs politiques et la violence dont elle s'accompagne.[4] (Bayart 1989: 287)

Neo-patrimonial or factional systems thrive in a variety of institutional forms, from multiparty electoral democracies to single- or non-party tyrannies. An example of the former is Nigeria. According to one authority, it manifests a 'prebendal' system that has much in common with neo-patrimonialism (Joseph 1987). Nigeria has never been subjected to personal rule because no ruler has yet been able to establish his hegemony at the centre.[5] Personal and factional loyalties do, however, permeate the system, and personal rulers have emerged on a regional basis. 'Prebendalism' refers to a pattern of political behaviour in which individuals compete for public offices in order to use them for the personal benefit of the office-holder and his faction. 'Clientelism' is the process of building up factional support on the basis of material pay-offs to clients. The two are obviously mutually supportive: 'To obtain and keep clients, one must gain a prebendal office; and to be sure that in the distribution of prebendal offices an individual or his kin have a reasonable chance of procuring one, clients must be gathered together to make their collective claim as well as to prove that the aspirant patron ... is a person of consequence whose co-optation would be rewarding ...' (Joseph 1987: 56–7). Nigeria's periodic return to electoral politics (1960–6 and 1979–83) revitalizes prebendalism by opening up an array of ministerial, sub-ministerial, and legislative offices at federal and state levels. As well, local and regional patrons enjoy increased leverage at the centre by channelling votes to appreciative national party leaders.

Neo-patrimonialism has also taken the wholly unfettered form of tyranny in sub-Saharan Africa. The most egregious examples are the Uganda of Idi Amin (1971–9), the Equatorial Guinea of Francesco Macias Nguema (1968–79), and the Central African Empire of Jean Bedel Bokassa (1966–79). Each of these regimes has been described as

[a] highly idiosyncratic, brutal, and personalist system of social repression set up by a civilian or military leader ... [T]yranny is the epitome of personal rule unfettered by moral constraints or political structures and unsupported by society. Although governmental structures may at times be retained, pro forma, all policy dictates derive directly from the personal dictator, no secondary loci of power are allowed to exist, and all of society is viewed as the personal fief and private domain of the dictator. (Decalo 1989: 4)

It is important to emphasize, however, that cultural and structural conditions do not determine a neo-patrimonial outcome. The lack of a single political culture, the weakness of national integration, the widespread poverty, the predominance of the peasantry, and the limited development of a class society – all these factors strain central institutions and encourage leaders to substitute personalistic authority, mercenary ties, and force for weakly legitimated institutions. But these conditions vary from country to country, as do the inclinations of leaders. Although Kenyan presidents Jomo Kenyatta and Daniel arap Moi have relished the monarchical role, former Tanzanian President Julius Nyerere abjured a personality cult in favour of the stance of a humble *mwalimu* (teacher).

Personal rule, though furnishing a time-worn, albeit uncertain, formula for governance under hostile conditions, is potentially economically destructive. Political logic drives insecure rulers and factional leaders at all levels to augment their capacity to reward followers (as well as themselves) and punish actual or potential opponents. Institutions – such as independent courts, public service commissions, auditors-general, bills of rights, a free press, autonomous legislatures, independent local governments, apolitical civil servants, open electoral systems, and democratically organized political parties – constrain their personal power to reward friends and destroy enemies. And so leaders desperately try to weaken these institutional constraints, in order more effectively to employ patronage, nepotism, and favouritism in appointments, promotions, and allocative and judicial decisions. Paradoxically, these efforts to centralize power in individuals render the state apparatus increasingly ineffectual, disorderly, and reliant on bribery and coercion. Hence, the short-term political rationality of personal and factional struggle not only wastes scarce resources, but also undermines administrative capacity and predictability, weakens other institutions and legal norms, and rewards unproductive or parasitical economic behaviour. These trends deter domestic and foreign investors by raising the costs and uncertainties of doing business, as described in Chapter 1.

Commentators on the economic problems of various African countries have alluded to aspects of this destructive political syndrome. In an article tellingly entitled 'Pirate Capitalism and the Inert Economy of Nigeria', an economist concludes that, '[f]or the most vigorous, capable, resourceful, well-connected, and "lucky" entrepreneurs ... productive economic activity, namely the creation of real income and wealth, has faded in appeal. Access to, and manipulation of, the government spending process has become the golden gateway to fortune' (Schatz 1984: 55).

An authority on Nimeiri's Sudan seeks to explain that country's comparatively early descent into economic crisis partly by reference to neo-patrimonial politics. In the late 1970s, this country received an influx of loans, aid, and direct foreign investment, mainly from Arab countries. Yet the opportunity for sustained growth was squandered. Although Sudan's investment programme suffered from economic weaknesses, it was also diverted by political exigencies – the need to pay 'for the clientelism on which the regime rested, and indeed for Nimeiri the personal ruler . . . It was not an act of God which had led to economic crisis before the drought, but the impact of Nimeiri's economic policies which had provided so many of the resources for his clientelistic politics' (Woodward 1987: 147). A Sudanese economist laments that this economically debilitating neo-patrimonial politics has persisted despite *coups d'état* and periodic democratic transitions. Therefore, a 'fundamental cause' of Sudan's continuing crisis is 'political' (Umbadda 1989: 23). Social indiscipline, patronage, nepotism, and corruption sabotage economic prospects. In particular, the

confinement of top professional jobs to inept/incompetent relatives and political supporters leads to the waste of talent and demoralization and exodus of competent staff. This summed up over time and institutions leads to gross mismanagement of the economy . . . negligence of priorities (regional, sectoral or institutional) and ultimately underdevelopment. Once such an attitude is institutionalized a government position does not become a responsibility, with accountability, but a prize to enjoy while it lasts. (Umbadda 1989: 22)

Another expert singles out a 'kleptocracy' for much of the blame for Sierra Leone's severe economic decline in the 1980s. A corrupt coterie destroyed the remaining democratic institutions in order to safeguard its ability to plunder the treasury and smuggle the country's precious metals. Self-serving policies and mismanagement drove peasants out of cash-crop production and into smuggling, and motivated even junior civil servants to demand bribes for official services (Zack-Williams 1990: 26). When Major-General Joseph Momoh assumed the presidency of this one-party state in late 1985, he therefore faced some difficult choices:

between the short-term requirements of a polity based upon kleptocracy, preferment, and patronage, and the long-term expectations of economic progress through investment in infrastructure, agricultural production, the resuscitation of diamond mining, and the utilisation of existing industrial capacity; and between the demands of external creditors and a potentially rebellious urban population. (Luke 1989: 136)

However, little changed after 1985; this provoked disillusioned intellectuals and popular movements to identify the system rather than the individual leader as the problem. This realization fuelled demands for a multiparty system in 1990 and 1991.

Hindsight suggests that these neopatrimonial tendencies had

wrought extensive economic damage by the mid-1970s in a few countries, notably Zaire, Uganda, Ghana, and Guinea. Elsewhere, as in Botswana, Côte d'Ivoire, Kenya, Tanzania, and Cameroon, shrewd political management kept these tendencies in check, and the state apparatus continued to function adequately. But the shocks of the late 1970s and early 1980s – soaring oil prices, drought, rising interest rates, and declining terms of trade – precipitated or accelerated a downward spiral of economic and political decay in many of these successful countries as well. Only a few states could cope effectively as foreign debts became unmanageable, foreign exchange shortfalls curtailed essential imports, public revenues fell, and poverty deepened. This debilitating politico-economic decline is now difficult to reverse.

Zambia is a case in point. A state-capitalist 'low-income developing country' of 8 million people in south-central Africa, it had a per capita gross national product of only $US290 in 1988. The country achieved considerable economic success from independence in 1964 until 1973, a success based upon the relatively high world price for the economy's mainstay, copper. However, the government missed its opportunity during this time: it markedly increased its expenditures on services, neglected agriculture, and failed to diversify the economy. (In 1990, copper still accounted for 85 per cent of total exports.) Economic difficulties thus soon surfaced when the price of copper fell in the mid-1970s and thereafter.

Falling living standards for all but the elite and a spiralling debt burden have characterized Zambia since 1973. From 1980 to 1987, per capita income declined at an annual rate of − 5.6 per cent – only war-torn Mozambique and tiny São Tomé and Principe have had worse records. Zambia's external debt reached $US8 billion by 1991. Obviously, the depressed world price for copper has featured centrally in the country's economic decline. Moreover, the repeated failure of the IMF and the World Bank to predict the persistence of low copper prices, along with the failure of donors to meet their aid pledges, have confounded recovery plans. But a bad situation has been turned into a disaster by inconsistent economic policy since the early 1980s, by ineffectual implementation of reform measures, and by politically inspired waste and mismanagement in the public sector.

President Kenneth Kaunda's system of personal rule until November 1991 must shoulder much of the blame for these governmental failings. First, Kaunda was chiefly responsible for the country's erratic and sometimes wrong-headed policy directions until the multiparty election of October 1991.[6] He made major policy decisions himself, and appointed and fired all important economic decision-makers. Further, the one-party state had stifled open debate of policy alternatives, though outspoken members of parliament had continued to criticize governmental corruption and mismanagement and defeat some bills. But the longstanding ban on opposition parties to the ruling United National Independence Party (UNIP) until late 1990, the requirement that parliamentary candidates receive the party's endorsement, and the president's vast powers of detention made sustained opposition difficult and risky.

Secondly, the clientelistic basis of the regime had wasted resources, fostered corruption, and foisted unqualified and redundant employees onto the civil service and multitudinous parastatals. To his credit, Kaunda had not relied upon massive repression. He had preferred to neutralize his opponents and retain his supporters by finding them public-sector or party jobs or opportunities to benefit from political connections. The auditor-general's report for 1986 discovered 'ample evidence of mismanagement of Government finances', and concluded that the government's financial accountability was 'meaningless' (quoted in Good 1989: 306). The report noted that accounting irregularities, the misappropriation of public funds, and unconstitutional or unauthorized expenditures were growing problems. Some political insiders had bought expensive imported automobiles with government loans, had easy access to scarce foreign exchange, and received overly generous housing and other allowances. 'Jobs for the boys' were found not only in government but in UNIP, which was bloated with full-time functionaries drawing salaries from public coffers. A central committee representative, a political secretary, a permanent secretary, chairpersons of the youth's and women's and other leagues, and two governors were found in each of the nine provinces. Each of the fifty-six districts had an equally confusing and overlapping set of UNIP offices. Many of these officials had access to an official car, a furnished house, and other perquisites.

Political practices such as these led one expert to the harsh view that

Zambia's acute malaise is a consequence chiefly of internal factors deriva-
tive of the single-party state and Kenneth Kaunda's personal rule. As
things stand, debt concessions and additional foreign aid would worsen
rather than improve the situation, since it would strengthen and encourage
an inefficient and authoritarian regime without bringing benefit to a majority of the people. Domestic reforms aimed at creating efficiency and
democratization in government, as well as the long-term diversification of
the economy, are the essentials for future development. (Good 1989: 298)

Zambia is currently again in the midst of a stabilization programme. An earlier one supported by the IMF in the mid-1980s was
brought to a halt by Kaunda in early 1987 following riots on the
Copperbelt instigated by increased food prices. The president
became a prominent critic of the social costs of IMF adjustment
programmes. At the urging of the international financial institutions
and aid donors, the government introduced in 1990 another stabilization package involving, among other policies, reduction in public
subsidies. Widespread rioting and looting and a near-successful
coup d'état in June 1990 did not this time shake Kaunda's resolve,
reinforced by the World Bank and IMF.

The evident public hostility to single-party rule compelled
Kaunda in mid-1990 to promise a referendum on the restoration of
multiparty democracy, and then in December 1990 to concede
multiparty elections without the referendum. A rising incidence of
child malnutrition, declining health services, the decay of educational institutions – while user-fees rose – and declining real
incomes fuelled popular resentments (Clark with Allison 1989:
46–50). In October 1991, Kaunda and UNIP went down to crushing
defeats in elections judged by external observers to be fair and open.
Frederick Chiluba, Chairman of the Zambian Congress of Trade
Unions and long-time critic of the regime, assumed the presidency
as leader of the Movement for Multiparty Democracy. Kaunda
gracefully ceded power.

Socialist experiments in Africa have also experienced 'false starts'.
Revolutionary Ethiopia, Mozambique, and Angola, and professedly or symbolically Marxist–Leninist Somalia, Benin, Congo, and
Madagascar confirm Paul Baran's maxim that 'socialism in backward and underdeveloped countries has a powerful tendency to
become a backward and underdeveloped socialism' (Baran 1957:9).
This tendency was most transparent in those regimes which, in the

absence of revolutionary struggle, simply declared themselves socialist. Guinea during the presidency of Sékou Touré (1958–84) is a good example. Under the guise of socialism, Touré headed a highly repressive, intrusive, and predatory state. Opponents were locked up, tortured, or driven into exile. Supporters were rewarded with sinecures in the civil service and state-owned corporations, with opportunities for corrupt dealings, and with privileged access to scarce goods in special shops and other perquisites. Smuggling and black-market activities mushroomed as the official economy fell apart.

Not even the revolutionary regimes, however, have been able to transform their societies. Socialist regimes in Ethiopia, Mozambique, and Angola have lacked effectiveness:

Given the state-centric orientation of a Marxist–Leninist worldview, the reality of the 'soft' state, with its inability to regulate and to implement public policy, comes as a continuing reminder of grave disappointment. For all their remarkable cohesion and sense of purpose, these regimes are limited in an organizational sense, unable fully to translate their strongly held socialist preferences into public policies. In appearance, these regimes seem centralized and unitary; in practice, however, they lack the capacity to penetrate the rural areas and to exercise the kind of leadership normally associated with a socialist transformation. (Rothchild and Foley 1987: 299)

The limited state capacities and indiscipline have stemmed from harsh socio-economic conditions, debilitating insurrections, and the lack of countervailing mass organizations. Economic backwardness shackles a country with a small and weak proletariat unable to check the oligarchic and personalistic tendencies of the revolutionary party. It also shackles the regime with paltry revenues with which to build a strong state apparatus, and with an invidious competition for scarce resources that undermines the solidarity of the party's cadre. These weaknesses, when combined with a Leninist 'vanguard' ideology and the insecurity induced by foreign-supported insurrections and/or economic pressures, have encouraged revolutionary elites to undertake an authoritarian revolution from above. In principle, when internal and external enemies are defeated and property relations transformed, society could begin to enjoy the socialist benefits of mass participation and control. In practice, however, that moment has not arrived. And the lack of open debate of major issues engendered egregious policy errors. These errors, compounded by a shortage of skilled personnel to manage complex centrally planned economies and by the costs of war and climatic disasters, have vitiated the state and induced widespread suffering in Ethiopia, Mozambique, and Angola.

In sum, these socialist governments have tried to collectivize agriculture and industry, extend services and control prices, but 'they have often only created a black market or simply killed production' (Ottaway 1987: 176).

Mozambique exemplifies this socialist incapacity. An East African country of 15 million, it won independence from Portugal in 1975 after a lengthy guerrilla struggle led by the Frelimo movement.

Following the official adoption of Marxism–Leninism in 1977, Frelimo set out to create a collectivized, planned economy. The government established and massively subsidized state farms on large plantations abandoned by Portuguese settlers. Advanced technology was to be used to increase output of foodstuffs and export crops on these state farms. Bureaucrats were authorized to set agricultural prices and manage the marketing system. Firms in the manufacturing and service sectors also came under state control. However, centralized planning with its emphasis on large-scale collective enterprises soon faltered.

The Mozambican state lacked the capacity to transform an underdeveloped peasant economy. First, by 1983, the main supporters of the collectivist drive had become the party–state apparatus itself. Frelimo, during a decade of anticolonial warfare, had developed a broad base of support – including poor peasants who objected to forced labour and forced cultivation practices, middle peasants and petty capitalists who resented the colonial privileges conferred upon the Portuguese settlers, and even some traditional elements who welcomed an end to Portuguese domination of social life (Hermele 1990: 3). Frelimo's strategy of socialist transformation, however, 'went further down the socialist road than the majority of peasants was prepared to accept' (Hermele 1990: 4), as well as alienating the petty capitalists and traditional rulers. Apathy and the burgeoning of the black market (which even the penalty of flogging failed to stem) contributed to the failure of the official strategy. Secondly, planning and state controls were weakened by a shortage of technocrats. This shortage grew ever more pronounced in the 1980s as the declining real incomes of civil servants drove many of the well-qualified ones into more lucrative alternative employment. Finally, periodic droughts and an intensification of Renamo-led insurrection under South African sponsorship wreaked economic havoc. By 1990, the war had destroyed much of the rural infrastructure of schools, clinics, community centres, shops, and electricity supplies, killed 900,000 people, displaced almost half of the rural population from their homes, spread malnutrition in a fertile country, and directed 40 per cent of government spending into the military (Ayisi 1991: 38; Green 1987: 27). Hence, by the mid-1980s, even the Frelimo leadership realized that central planning was 'largely illusory' (Wuyts 1989: 5).

A sympathetic account of the situation in Mueda, a district in the far north of the country, illustrates the desperateness of the situation as early as 1983. An observer discovered:

a national government ridden by demands of a complex economy, plagued by the effect of oil crises and destabilisation, held back by the lack of cadres, infrastructure and communication. In the liberated areas [during the struggle], the peasants had a voice and Frelimo understood how to answer. In independent Mozambique, the voice of the peasants is weaker and the government has neither the means nor always the understanding to answer ... Where the government fails to assume its responsibility, the local community has to do it.

Local communities in fact had largely to fend for themselves. In the village of Nandimba, people were

embarrassed ... at the lack of decent clothing for the children at school and for themselves ... They look around for traditional methods of making soap and use whatever scrap metal is available to try and make knives and hoes. The gains [of independence] have to be formulated in other terms: political freedom, self-determination, democratic rule. By 1983, these gains were disputable. The institutions had been created and the formal framework of guidelines formulated. But this was not enough. Materially and politically, conditions were not yet there. (Egero 1987: 169, 165)

Under these conditions, Frelimo shifted ground at its Fourth Congress in 1983. It dismantled many state farms, distributed land to peasants, and sought to encourage peasant production by shifting resources to the household sector and raising agricultural prices. Nonetheless, the situation continued to deteriorate: GNP declined at an annual rate of 7 per cent in 1982–6 (*IMF Survey* 16 Dec. 1991).

What could be done? Africa's Marxist–Leninist states have had little choice but to jettison their 'backward' socialism. Even their erstwhile patron, the Soviet Union, had urged accommodations with their domestic opponents and the international financial institutions. To end internal wars and gain credits and assistance from multilateral and bilateral development agencies, revolutionary Angola, Mozambique, and Ethiopia have all renounced Marxism–Leninism. And they have all undertaken to retrench and liberalize their economies, and reform their political systems. Angola's MPLA government, for instance, offered many of its state-owned plantations for sale in 1990, and in 1991 it pledged to free prices and wages, privatize a range of public corporations, and encourage private investment. It also negotiated an agreement with its insurgent adversary, UNITA, to hold multiparty elections in 1992.

As for Frelimo, its Fifth Congress in July 1989 signalled a major reorientation. It dropped its Marxist–Leninist designation, declared itself a 'vanguard of all the people' (rather than only of the workers and peasants), invited businessmen to join the party, listened to addresses by religious leaders, and defended the unpopular Economic Recovery Programme which the government had negotiated with the IMF and World Bank in 1986–7. In 1990, Frelimo introduced an amended constitution that dropped the designation 'People's Republic', guaranteed basic civil rights (including freedom of the press and universal adult suffrage), recognized the right to own private property, and legalized opposition parties. After signing a partial ceasefire with Renamo in December 1990, the government scheduled competitive party elections for July 1991. These were later postponed to 1992.

Revolutionary socialist movements thus confront daunting challenges; yet their decline into authoritarianism and economic failure is not inevitable. The Eritrean People's Liberation Front (EPLF), for example, may avoid this outcome in its homeland, if Eritreans vote to separate from Ethiopia in a referendum scheduled for 1993. Eritrea shares the endemic poverty of many of its neighbours. But it has certain advantages. First, the Marxist guerrilla movements that have waged war for over twenty years have fought for political liberty as well as national liberation. They have forged cohesive movements and popular followings on the basis of opposition to tyrannical rule from Addis Ababa. 'Eritreans see their revolution as one against the unjust use of power by a colonial regime that has destroyed all their national and democratic freedoms' (Pateman 1990: 457). The EPLF's democratic commitments, moreover, are not merely rhetorical: diverse visitors to the EPLF zones in the

1980s commented upon the egalitarian, fraternal, and non-authoritarian relations of Eritrean society and the guerrilla movement. Secondly, the EPLF has apparently drawn lessons from the decline of other socialist movements in Africa and elsewhere. It allows free and open discussion within the movement, and contemplates the installation of a multiparty system. It accepts a mixed economy, having observed the abject failure of Addis Ababa's command economy. It has not forced collectivization upon the peasants in the process of land reform. And it has accorded women a prominent place both as fighters and front members. Finally, with the collapse of the Cold War, Eritrea may be spared the destructive intervention of outside powers that has vitiated other socialist experiments.

It is thus conceivable that some socialist movements may surmount the onerous socio-economic and political circumstances to represent a genuinely democratic and efficient option.

Africa's post-colonial experience suggests a strong reciprocal relationship between state decay and economic crisis. The degeneration of the will and/or capacity of governmental organizations has aggravated or instigated economic problems; conversely, economic decline has impeded state capacity-building. Economic recovery will require the rebuilding and reorienting of governance.

To appreciate what is involved in this enterprise, consider the generic obstacles and dilemmas which prospective state-builders confront. They will need to overcome or diminish fiscal, bureaucratic, and political weaknesses in a context of economic crisis and restraint.

First, in the late 1970s, a *fiscal crisis* materialized in many sub-Saharan countries as declining public revenues encountered a governmental reluctance to reduce expenditures. These countries' principal source of public revenues is export–import taxes (see Table 1), especially levies on one or a handful of primary commodity exports. Income and profit taxes are rarely a major contributor to public coffers, owing to the limited number of enumerated income and profit earners and the opportunities for tax evasion where tax investigators are few and corruptible (e.g., Ogbonna 1975: 53–61; and Nellis 1972). (Where a handful of large corporations dominate extractive industries, however, royalties and taxes on profits are often a major source of revenue.) Land taxes are difficult to administer in societies where ownership is often unclear

Table 1. *Sources of central governments' current revenue (% of total)*

	taxes on income, profit and capital gain		domestic taxes on goods and services		taxes on international trade and transactions		non-tax revenue	
	1972	1987 or 1988	1972	1987 or 1988	1972	1987 or 1988	1972	1987 or 1988
Ethiopia	23	30	30	22	30	19	11	26
Burkina Faso	17	12	18	14	52	34	10	26
Malawi	31	34	24	33	20	16	24	17
Zaire	22	27	13	15	58	43	4	14
Mali	–	8	–	22	–	28	4	9
Uganda	22	6	33	25	36	70	9	0
Burundi	18	–	18	–	40	–	7	–
Tanzania	30	26	29	57	22	9	19	5
Togo	–	36	–	10	–	35	–	10
Somalia	11	–	25	–	45	–	14	–
Central African Republic	18	24	–	13	–	45	–	6
Rwanda	18	–	14	–	42	–	8	–
Kenya	36	27	20	41	24	19	19	10
Zambia	50	38	20	40	14	17	16	4
Sierra Leone	33	20	15	22	42	57	10	3
Sudan	12	–	30	–	41	–	16	–
Lesotho	14	11	2	10	63	68	11	11
Ghana	18	29	29	28	41	35	11	8
Senegal	18	–	25	–	31	–	3	–
Chad	17	–	12	–	45	–	5	–
Liberia	41	34	20	25	32	35	5	4
Zimbabwe	–	47	–	25	–	15	–	12
Nigeria	43	40	26	5	18	7	13	63
Botswana	20	43	2	1	47	14	30	42
Cameroon	–	31	–	15	–	19	–	26
Congo, People's Republic	19	–	40	–	27	–	8	–

Note: rows do not add to 100 because minor sources of revenue are excluded.
Source: World Bank, *World Development Report 1990*, Table 12.

because of customary arrangements circumscribing land tenure. Thus, levies on primary commodity exports typically generate, in one form or another, from one-quarter to one-half of public revenues. In oil- exporting economies such as Nigeria's, or in copper-exporting economies such as Zambia's, the extractive sector accounts for well over half the government's income in the form of taxes on employees' incomes and corporate profits, royalties, and export duties.

Cyclical swings in commodity prices have had a disastrous effect on budgets (as well as on external accounts). During the era of commodity price rises in the 1970s, most governments increased expenditures proportionately, or more so. The collapse of commodity prices at the end of the decade instigated fiscal crises for governments committed to ambitious projects with high recurrent costs. In Nigeria, for instance, federal revenues rose more than nine-fold between 1970–1 and 1976–7 as the price of oil escalated, from 756 million naira to 7,070 million naira. With the collapse of the oil price six years later, Nigeria's revenues fell back to near their earlier level. This created a severe adjustment problem, for private banks were no longer interested in lending money to help Nigeria service its large external debt and high recurrent expenses. To make matters worse, world demand for most of Africa's primary exports is not expected to grow more than marginally in the 1990s.

Of course, not all countries fell into what the World Bank refers to as a 'commodity cycle trap'; Cameroon and Botswana managed their boom revenues prudently. Cameroon used much of the extra revenues from the oil boom in 1979–81 to repay its external debt. Public spending in Botswana fell as a share of GDP during the diamond boom of the 1980s. Adjusting to the downswing in world prices was thus much easier in these two countries than in most of the rest.

Not only did commodity prices fall, but the marketed output of smallholders' export crops (and therefore tax receipts) also plummeted in many countries. Low producer prices, delays in crop payments, unreliable marketing systems, and the unavailability of consumer goods discouraged producers. Marketing boards have been a major instrument for squeezing surplus out of the smallholders. Created during the colonial period to stabilize the producers' price, these boards were soon converted into milch cows for governments. The imperial powers extracted resources in the 1940s and

1950s by borrowing funds from the boards at highly favourable rates of interest. Marketing boards continued to supply governments with income following independence, both in the form of concessional loans, often unrepaid, and taxes. The effective level of taxation on export crops was until recently very high. In Ghana, for instance, the government's share of cocoa sales revenue rose from 3 per cent in 1947–8 to 60 per cent in 1978–9 (World Bank 1983: 83). Government exactions together with expensive marketing arrangements and overvalued currencies had reduced the return to producers to a fraction of the world price by the end of the 1970s (World Bank 1988b: 91).

The producers' response has been to switch production to more lucrative commodities or smuggle their highly-taxed crops into neighbouring countries offering higher returns. Up to half of Ghana's cocoa crop was smuggled into Côte d'Ivoire and Togo in the early 1980s, and Zaire lost at least $US300 million in revenues through the smuggling of coffee in 1976 alone (Young and Turner 1986: 246). However, officially recorded cocoa production has grown markedly in Ghana since the inauguration of structural adjustment in 1983. Ghana's 'Economic Recovery Programmes' have boosted producer prices and the availability of imports, lowered the rate of inflation, reduced the costs of marketing cocoa, and facilitated a more realistic exchange rate.

Not all governments were as heavy-handed in their dealings with peasants as the pre-1983 Ghanaian governments. The Ivorian government until 1989, for example, adroitly managed to extract revenues from primary producers without discouraging production. La Caisse de Stabilisation et de Soutien des Prix des Productions Agricoles, created in 1962 by the amalgamation of two existing boards, is responsible for stabilizing the prices of various commodities – coffee, cocoa, bananas, palm oil, copra, tobacco and cashew nuts. This board has been the principal contributor to the government's investment programme in agricultural diversification and manufacturing. The government took an annual average of 38 per cent of the cocoa fob price and 31 per cent of the coffee price in the 1970s. About 50 per cent of the fob price went to the producers and 12–14 per cent to the intermediaries, processors, traders, and transporters (Marcussen and Torp 1982: 70–2). La Caisse procured significant resources for the government and still maintained high, and even increasing, output by ensuring that producer prices at least kept pace with inflation and that a reasonably efficient marketing system operated (Hecht 1983: 26–34). However, the board began to produce high deficits after the mid-1980s as the government, for political reasons, persisted in paying cocoa producers at the same level as coffee producers, even though world prices for cocoa had collapsed. Producer prices were not dramatically adjusted downwards until 1989.

For sub-Saharan Africa, the collapse of tax revenues has engendered severe adjustment problems. Owing to the unavailability of commercial loans, governments have become very dependent on foreign aid; this amounted to 12.2 per cent of sub-Saharan Africa's GNP in 1986 (World Bank 1988b: 75). Most governments have had no option but to reduce budget deficits by cutting their expenditures – though this has not been easy.

Public expenditures rose sharply following independence, reflecting the statist approach to development of regimes whether professedly capitalist or socialist. The governments' expansive economic and social roles boosted the growth of public employment. This commonly increased at a rate two or three times that of population; annual rates of growth of central government employment as high as 14 or 15 per cent were recorded in Zaire, Ghana, and Tanzania for certain periods in the 1960s, 1970s, or early 1980s.[7] Regionally, employment in regular-line agencies of central and local government grew by an estimated 240 per cent in the twenty years following 1960 – from 1.9 to 6.5 million. If non-financial parastatal organizations are included, public employment climbed by about 160 per cent in this period, to a total of about 10 million. By 1980, the public sector accounted for half of those in non-agricultural wage employment (Abernethy 1988: 189).

Overstaffing sometimes reached major proportions. In one West African country, a consultant concluded that 6,000 of 6,800 headquarters staff in two ministries were redundant (World Bank 1983: 103). Censuses of their civil services carried out by the Central African Republic and Guinea in the mid-1980s discovered that 1,300 and 7,000 employees respectively were 'phantom workers' – bogus employees whose salaries were pocketed by those in on the scam (World Bank 1988b: 116). In Cameroon, the civil service roughly *doubled* in size within several years of Paul Biya's accession to the presidency in 1983. Biya was motivated by political considerations: he felt he had to buttress his position by finding jobs for the many unemployed university and secondary school graduates from his home area of southern Cameroon. But the consequent overstaffing presented a major problem with the decline of the price for oil and then economic recession in 1987 (*West Africa* 13–19 June 1989: 1890–2).

Recent adjustment programmes aim to equilibrate revenues and expenditures mainly by squeezing the latter. If cuts have to be made, state managers have been more likely to prune capital and maintenance costs than other items (Hicks 1991: 29–35). External debt service has grown – usually to a third or more of current public revenue – but this expenditure is unavoidable, barring a unilateral moratorium on debt payments or a multilateral agreement on debt relief. Significant reductions in the defence budget are unlikely because, where governmental authority is shaky, political leaders are wary of alienating the armed forces. Governments are also reluctant to cut public employment. The very identity of the state is bound up with the administrative apparatus. In the outlying districts, the only symbols of the state may be the local government offices, with the national flag flying out front, and an army detachment. Also, the public sector generally plays an important role in servicing the patron–client networks on which the political elite's survival largely depends.

As economic decline depresses middle-class living standards and exacerbates political discontent, the rulers fight reducing patronage to fickle supporters in the state apparatus. Civil servants are generally well-placed to demonstrate their anger. When President Houphouet-Boigny of Côte d'Ivoire announced, in early 1990, salary cuts for civil servants to cope with a revenue shortfall and a heavy debt service burden, the response was a wave of strikes and demonstrations. For the first time, demonstrators called for the resignation of the venerable president, and dozens of teachers were arrested during a March riot in Abidjan. Contemporaneous governmental attempts to establish income guidelines or low national minimum wages in Nigeria, Ghana, and Zaire also provoked strong anti-government protests (*West Africa* 26 Mar.–1 Apr. 1990: 479; *West Africa* 3–10 Sept. 1990: 2410).

Although something must be done to reduce public expenditures, donor pressures to declare numerous civil servants redundant may go too far. An economistic perspective sees only waste and redundancy in a high public-sector wage bill. Administrative apparatuses, however, do not serve only the end of economic efficiency; they are valuable as well as 'employers of last resort' in countries where widespread unemployment and discontent threaten political order and national unity.

On the revenue side, adjustment policies have posed a perplexing dilemma. On the one hand, effective taxation rates of 50 per cent or more deterred primary producers from increasing or even maintaining agricultural output. On the other hand, export taxes were a major source of public revenue in most countries. The World Bank and other international agencies have pressed a reduction in export taxes in order to channel more returns to agricultural producers. But how could governments reduce burgeoning budget deficits and massive external debts at the same time as they surrendered an important part of their revenues? Low world prices and the lead-time needed to increase production of some crops have generated a dismal fiscal position. 'Even for crops where the price elasticity of supply is very high, and where the revenues arising from increased sales would partly – or even fully – compensate the public sector for lower tax rates, the lag in supply response for most crops must imply that the short-term effects on public revenues would be strongly negative' (Colclough 1985: 42). Until world commodity prices rise, the prospect of solving the fiscal crisis is meagre.

Meanwhile, the budgetary cutbacks weakened the state and made production costly by depriving producers of reliable public services. Roads, railways, water, power, and telephone systems deteriorated. In countries such as Nigeria, manufacturers have had to resort to private power generators – at enormous expense – owing to the costly assembly-line disruptions caused by periodic power failures. Businesses have also invested in private courier and communications systems and wasted their managers' time in needless face-to-face discussions owing to the poor quality of telephones. And the unreliability of public transit in Nigerian cities has compelled large companies to provide their own transport for workers. In addition, supplies to all public services have suffered: classrooms lack textbooks and even chalk; health clinics and hospitals lack vaccines and medicines; agricultural extension workers and field officers lack means of transport or, if these are available, lack fuel or spare parts, and thus cannot do their jobs; and so on. The morale, honesty, and efficiency of civil servants have therefore declined. And once counterproductive patterns are established, they are difficult to change.

The fiscal crisis is thus reciprocally related to what some saw as a *crisis of administrative capacity*. 'Crisis' was not too strong a word if it was true, as former World Bank president Robert S. McNamara declared in 1985, that 'a number of previously able and functioning institutions are now losing their effectiveness'. He warned of

entire central ministries that are no longer in adequate control of their budgets and personnel, public agencies that have lost their capacity to carry out their proper tasks, state universities, scientific facilities, and statistical offices that have seriously declined in the quality of their work, parastatal organizations and marketing boards that impede rather than promote productivity, and critically important agricultural research institutions that are becoming increasingly ineffective. (McNamara 1985: 9)

Yet this picture is misleading insofar as administrative capacity varies widely. At one extreme are countries like Uganda, Zaire, and Guinea which saw in the 1970s a virtual collapse of their civil services and professional standards. At the other are a few countries like Botswana, Zimbabwe, Mauritius, and to a lesser extent Côte d'Ivoire and Cameroon which have maintained effective bureaucracies. Most countries fall somewhere in between.

Two processes impinge on the capacity of the public service. One is the politicization of the bureaucracy attendant upon a growing resort to patrimonial mechanisms of rule. The other is the squeeze placed on the salaries, perquisites, and facilities of civil servants as revenues shrink and external agencies press governments to reduce budget deficits. Both processes, unless carefully managed, vitiate administrative effectiveness.

Consider the impact on public administration of the emergence of neo-patrimonial governance. Bureaucracy at independence was vulnerable as office-holders had not had time to develop a distinctive *ésprit de corps*. It degenerated into patrimonial administration unless the supreme leader shielded it from the corrosive impact of patron–client politics. Often, however, the presidential-monarch treated the administration as his personal property. He or his lieutenants selected the top administrators on the basis of personal loyalties and assigned their tasks as they saw fit. The public officials, in turn, 'treat their administrative work for the ruler as a personal service based on their duty of obedience and respect' (Bendix 1962: 345). The ruler may even have permitted his officials to act arbitrarily and corruptly, provided this behaviour did not breed rebellion. Consequently, the bureaucratic virtues of hierarchical authority, expertise, neutrality, predictability, and efficiency were eroded.

Even Tanzania, a country noted for the probity of its top leadership, has suffered from what a Tanzanian academic graphically labels 'bureaucratic feudalism' (Munishi 1989: 153–67). This denotes a pervasive patron–client system. Political patrons secure positions in the civil service and parastatals for clients, who then owe loyalty to these patrons rather than to their hierarchical superiors. These transorganizational factions advance the interests of their members – often to the detriment of the public they are supposed to serve. Hence, 'without accountability, both foreign aid and internal surpluses will be deflected to the nodes of power in the political system at the expense of popular socioeconomic development' (Munishi 1989: 166).

Yet this was not the invariable outcome. In Côte d'Ivoire, for example, bureaucratization had been relatively successful until the end of the 1980s. This success was due to a consistent policy of President Houphouet-Boigny and his stable coterie of lieutenants: to Africanize the public service slowly and ensure that key positions were filled with qualified applicants who had satisfied the high standards of a French-dominated secondary and post-secondary educational system. This, together with appropriate incentives and accountability, had permitted the socialization of public servants into bureaucratic norms and values:

Given the natural tendency toward inertia, the longer a structure survives the more difficult it is to disrupt. In Côte d'Ivoire the deliberate policy of maintaining [the bureaucracy's] continuity with the colonial past meant that the disintegration and weakening of bureaucratic values and procedures, caused elsewhere by rapid Africanization and political penetration, would have been avoided. The significance of the expatriate presence did not derive from the occupation of executive positions as such, but from the continuity of institutional procedures and 'agency ideologies' which they ensured. (Crook 1988: 23)

However, the ravages of economic crisis and patron–client politics had begun to unravel the integrity and efficiency of even the Ivoirien bureaucracy by 1990.

When corruption, nepotism, inefficiency, and arbitrariness reach the levels found in Uganda, Zaire, Guinea, and Nigeria, unrestrained personalistic politics is a principal cause and must be reformed. Elsewhere, however, a neo-patrimonialism has furnished a minimal basis for governance without bringing an economy to ruin. There is an acute dilemma: patronage is wasteful and fosters incompetence and unpredictability; but if patronage flows are severely reduced, governance in many cases would rest more heavily on repression – heightening human suffering and undermining an already tenuous national integration – or succumb to political instability. Whether technocratic or clientelistic criteria should prevail in particular appointments, promotions, and allocations is thus an issue that is not easily resolved.

The other damaging process is the shrinking of the salaries and amenities of public servants since the 1970s. Since it is politically suicidal for rulers to dismiss many civil servants in a context of massive unemployment and poverty, governments have retained most of their employees while allowing inflation to erode their real incomes. This reconciles political realities with the need to reduce budgetary deficits. But the decline of civil servants' salaries can be devastating (as mentioned in Chapter 1). In most sub-Saharan countries, middle-level officials cannot even feed – let alone adequately house, clothe, and educate – their families on their salaries. In Sudan, basic starting salaries fell by four-fifths between 1970 and 1983, while in Ghana and Uganda, real starting salaries had fallen below subsistence level by 1983 (World Bank 1988b: 115). In Guinea, the average salary in the civil service was the equivalent of only $US18 per month in 1985 (Picard and Graybeal 1988: 11).

Staff morale, honesty, and efficiency usually decline along with real compensation. Without the facilities or tools to do their jobs efficiently, many civil servants simply become time-servers. Or they turn to bribes, embezzlement of public funds, and/or moonlighting in order to supplement their meagre salaries and benefits. In Uganda, 'the system of official remuneration has the consequence of putting on sale public employees to the highest bidder' (Mamdani 1988: 1166). In Guinea, '[w]ith the devaluation of the syli and the low level of functionary salaries, there developed a system of "Ye Dogho" ... or parallel side payments ... for virtually all governmental services' (Picard and Graybeal 1988: 6). Some Guinean public servants earned ten times their salaries through bribes, kickbacks, and embezzlement in 1985, according to a World Bank estimate (ibid. 1988: 11). The spectacular degree of administrative corruption in Zaire and Nigeria is widely documented. It is also common for officials to be unavailable during working hours because they are attending to their private business affairs, often informal-sector activities. To survive in many countries, civil servants must use their ingenuity to generate supplementary incomes. Moonlighting that involves animal husbandry, poultry or foodstuff farming, or urban transport can be productive and socially useful. But the costs include reduced administrative efficiency and public disenchantment with unavailable or unresponsive civil servants.

Inadequate public salaries and other problems, especially urban lawlessness and physical insecurity, also spawn or exacerbate shortages of qualified professional and technical staff. Most African civil services cannot find qualified applicants to fill vacancies for engineers, managers, accountants, economists, and doctors. In Nigeria, a survey in 1977 found that vacancy rates for scientists, secondary school teachers, and other professionals all exceeded 40 per cent (World Bank 1988b: 103). So serious did the loss of professional staff become that President Ibrahim Babangida appointed a Presidential Task Force on the Brain Drain in October 1988. The more experienced staff evidently quit or avoid the public service in order to seek employment abroad or in the private sector. Ghana, Ethiopia, and Uganda have perhaps been the worst affected by a 'brain drain' of qualified professionals. A widespread decline in the quality of secondary and university education in the 1980s aggravated the problem of finding qualified staff. Economic crisis and budgetary cutbacks have deprived educational institutions of the resources they require; hence, buildings and equipment have deteriorated, many distinguished faculty have departed, and curricula have become dated as instructors lose touch with thinking in their fields.

The lack of a cadre of well-trained indigenous economists and financial experts is particularly troubling for governments contemplating economic reform. Who is going to advise political leaders on the available economic options and strategies? The answer often is: expatriate economists under technical assistance programmes, or protégés of the World Bank trained in neo-classical economics at elite Western universities. This is unsatisfactory, however, as many foreign and local technocrats lack an intimate knowledge of, or sensitivity to, local social, cultural, and political conditions. Their advice, though pleasing to foreign agencies, is therefore unlikely to be attuned to political and social realities. These limitations of the technobureaucracy may further constrain economic recovery.

Economic crisis also has negative repercussions for the *political capacity* of states, in particular their ability to mobilize popular support behind governmental programmes. Willing compliance is the only sure basis for a stable and effective government. As consent declines, so too does the governability of a society in which the coercive force at the centre is meagre or unreliable. This has been the unhappy story of many sub-Saharan countries.

One indicator of a state's limited political capacity is a high incidence of political violence. African countries have suffered far more war and war-related deaths since 1960 (when many African colonies became independent) than other regions of the Third World with larger populations. 'War deaths' – those resulting from 'any armed conflict which includes one or more governments, and causes the deaths of 1,000 or more people per year' (Sivard 1987: 28) – comprise deaths from both internal wars (national liberation struggles, revolts, insurrections, rebellions, revolutions, and civil wars) and wars between states. An estimated 4.5 million people died from these political causes in sub-Saharan Africa (excluding South Africa and Namibia) in 1960–87. In the same period, war and war-related deaths claimed 330,000 in Latin America, 41,000 in India, and 55,000 in China.[8]

Civil wars and insurrections have taken the major toll in lives and ruined economies. *Coups d'état* have been plentiful – one study of Tropical Africa is provocatively entitled 'Sixty Coups in Thirty Years' (McGowan and Johnson 1986) – though most of these have been 'palace coups' with low human and (direct) economic costs. Benin holds the record with six successful coups, closely followed by Ghana, Uganda, and Sudan. For each successful coup, there are generally three or four unsuccessful attempts and foiled plots. Inter-state wars (e.g., those between Somalia and Ethiopia in 1977, and Tanzania and Uganda in 1978–9) have been rare and much less costly than wars of national liberation (in particular, those in the Portuguese territories before 1975, and Zimbabwe until 1979) and, above all, civil wars. Table 2 indicates that civil wars and insurrections accounted for almost 4 million of the 4.5 million African lives lost in large-scale political violence. Scattered riots and communal violence and flagrant official violations of human rights (as recorded in periodic reports of Amnesty International and Africa Watch) are further manifestations of hegemonic crisis in many countries.

In extreme cases, African populations have been subjected to every form of political violence. In Uganda, an early indicator of the troubles that lay ahead was an army mutiny in 1964, only two years after independence. This was followed in 1966 by a constitutional crisis in which Prime Minister Milton Obote carried through a coup against the Baganda by dismissing the Muganda president, Edward Mutesa, assuming all presidential powers, and terminating the federal system which favoured Buganda. Further coups followed. In January 1971, General Idi Amin Dada and his West Nile supporters overthrew President Obote, and then massacred the latter's Langi and Acholi supporters within the armed forces. In July 1985, General Tito Okello and his Acholi followers in the army ejected Obote, supported by his Langi tribesmen, from the presidency for the second time. Political assassination and torture were widely practiced by Idi Amin during his eight years in power, and continued under the second Obote government from December 1980 until July 1985. A full-scale civil war broke out in 1979 as Obote's army invaded Uganda from Tanzania. With Tanzanian support, Obote's forces overthrew Amin. Insurrections have continued unabated since 1979, though the main protagonists and intensity of conflict have varied. Yoweri Museveni's National Resistance Army defeated

Table 2. *Civil war deaths in sub-Saharan Africa (deaths in 1000s)*

Country	Opponents	Date	Deaths
Angola	UNITA	1975–87	213
Burundi	Hutu/Tutsi	1972	100
Chad	various	1980–7	7
Ethiopia	Eritrea	1974–87	546[a]
Mozambique	Renamo	1981–7	401[a]
Nigeria	Biafra	1967–70	2,000
Sudan	North/South	1963–72	500
Sudan	North/South	1984–7	10
Uganda	various	1981–7	102
Zaire	Katanga	1960–5	100
Zimbabwe	Ndebele	1983	2
TOTAL			3,981

Note: [a] includes war-induced famine deaths.
Source: Calculated from data in Sivard 1987: 31.

General Okello's forces in January 1986. Since then, the security situation and the human rights record have gradually improved. Chad, Liberia, Sudan, Equatorial Guinea, Mozambique, Angola, Ethiopia, and Somalia have had similarly violent histories.

What accounts for the disturbing record of discord that afflicts so many African states? Colonialism is implicated, directly in that many deaths resulted from national liberation struggles, and indirectly in that the colonies were conquered territories that arbitrarily grouped diverse cultural-linguistic groups within common boundaries. This, in conjunction with the uneven regional impress of development and the politicization of ethnic identities by ambitious politicians, fostered the regional/ethnic hostilities which, at their worst, can degenerate into civil wars. The other exogenous factor is the willingness of external powers to 'fish in troubled waters'. Foreign interventions, both overt and covert, have exacerbated local conflicts and regional wars in Ethiopia, Somalia, Chad, Zaire, Mozambique, Angola, Lesotho, and Zimbabwe.

But it was the fact that national governments did not command the loyalty of many of their citizens that permitted foreign intrigues. Consent is firm when it has a normative basis in a legitimating ideology; however, ideologies are unlikely to be persuasive in the absence of the appropriate material conditions. If the ruled are to consent to their subordinate position within a social order, they must believe that it satisfies their minimum material interests. Yet, as suggested earlier, the ruling groups in post-colonial African countries have rarely succeeded in fashioning effective legitimating formulas. Prolonged economic contractions thus threaten their hold on power. Public disaffection grows with falling real wages and diminishing returns from cash crops, rising unemployment and underemployment, escalating prices, shortages of essential commodities, and deteriorating public services.

The austerity introduced as part of structural adjustment programmes has often undermined further a government's popular support. These political costs could have been minimized if the international financial institutions and the developed countries had transferred sufficient resources to cushion the welfare consequences of the stabilization policies they demanded. Instead, governments had to weather the storm. In the late 1980s, the cities were the main site of public demonstrations of hostility to governments and their adjustment programmes. Disaffection also took a regional-ethnic dimension where decline was regionally uneven and the rulers hailed disproportionately from the prosperous regions. Insurrectional tendencies in the poorer regions emerged as the decline in public revenues and consequent deterioration of the transport and communications systems weakened the state's coercive arm.

Not only did economic decline heighten pressures toward state disintegration; political chaos in turn aggravated economic problems. Private investors fled. Agricultural production plummeted. Financing the military machine and repairing war damage drained scarce resources from essential public services and capital investments. Whereas military expenditures accounted in 1984 for an average 3.0 per cent of GNP in sub-Saharan Africa as a whole, defence ate up a far higher proportion in countries engaged in internal wars: 14.2 per cent of GNP in Angola, 10.4 per cent in Chad, 9.3 per cent in Ethiopia, 4.8 per cent in Mozambique, and 6.2 per cent in Zimbabwe (which committed 12,000 troops to securing a rail corridor through Mozambique to Beira) (Sivard 1987: 45). Severe budget and balance of payments deficits have resulted.

In extreme cases, as in Mozambique, Ethiopia, Sudan, Somalia, Uganda, Angola, Liberia, and Chad, civil wars eviscerated faltering economies. Mozambique's war disrupted production and transport in the middle and late 1980s to the extent that 80 per cent of visible and invisible exports were lost. The dislocation of almost half of the country's rural population – 4.5 million people – has decimated agricultural output. And defence has absorbed 40 per cent of government spending (Green 1987: 7). Unfortunately, the macroeconomic costs of war in Mozambique and the other countries outweighed even those of inappropriate policies, drought, and shifts in the international terms of trade. And when drought coincides with insurrection, famines result even in countries with fertile and abundant land.

In less extreme cases of political disorder, insurgency shades off into banditry or isolated rebellions – as in Senegal (Casamance), Sierra Leone, Uganda, Rwanda, Burundi, or Zaire in the past few years. The macro-economic and human costs are not as severe, though the general insecurity and incapacity of the state impede economic recovery.

Political incapacity and economic decline are thus closely linked; a precondition for economic recovery where disorder prevails is social peace. Structural adjustment programmes cannot succeed in the context of a civil war, since they can only be implemented – and then merely partially – in secure areas around cities and towns (see, e.g., Ottaway 1988).

It has been difficult to devise the formulas for resolving these conflicts and generating consent. By 1990, the demise of the Cold War had removed the incentive for East and West to support opposing sides with weapons and economic aid. Soviet–US cooperation laid the basis for the resolution of the destructive civil wars in Angola and Ethiopia in 1991. Still, the brutal wars in Sudan, Somalia, Mozambique, Chad and Liberia, and less intense insurrections elsewhere, continued. In a continent dominated by authoritarian rule, many came to hope that democracy could furnish the institutions capable of peacefully resolving these conflicts and building consent. Democratization may indeed offer more hope than the existing discredited systems, but Africa's problems are so intractable that democracy too may founder.

Both capitalist and socialist success require an effective state oriented by the extrinsic discipline of a hegemonic class or the self-discipline of a nationalistic or revolutionary elite. This is obvious in the case of contemporary socialism. Its emphasis upon public ownership, central planning, and bureaucratic controls assumes an expert and highly motivated state apparatus capable of collecting detailed economic data, acting consistently in an instrumental-rational manner, and securing the compliance of the population. The centrality of an effective state is less obvious in the liberal, market-oriented approach advocated by the World Bank and the IMF. But, even here, the state, though operating within a narrow sphere, is crucial. Structural adjustment assumes an institutional capacity and will to design and implement complex policies concerning prices, trade, banking, finance, and foreign investment, to reform parastatals, and to manage complicated negotiations with donors and the subsequent assistance programmes. Also, markets do not spontaneously come into being. They only operate satisfactorily within a particular political, administrative, infra-structural, and legal framework – what the World Bank calls an 'enabling environment'. If this enabling environment does not obtain, it must be created, and this is the role of the state.

A facsimile of a modern capitalist state was bequeathed by the departing colonial powers in countries where decolonization was relatively peaceful. But this prototype invariably underwent modifications in the 1960s and 1970s as political structures adapted – or failed to adapt – to prevailing social and material conditions. Where personalistic dictatorships or breakdowns into political chaos occurred, economic decline soon followed. However, most governmental organizations maintained adequate levels of services and social order until the late 1970s. It was the current economic crisis, driven by climatic disasters, environmental deterioration, inimical global economic trends, as well as unsatisfactory policies and politics, that overwhelmed the coping capacity of fragile states. Today, fiscal, administrative, and hegemonic crises impede economic reform and recovery in many countries.

If revolutionary experiments and state-capitalism have not offered a shortcut to progress, can the currently popular liberal-democratic approach offer a practicable way forward? In theory, this approach should regenerate in popularly elected governments a reformist political will and heightened political and administrative capacities. This is the proposition we must now begin to examine.

§ 3 §

CREATING AND ENABLING
LIBERAL STATES

Today a liberal-democratic ethos infuses the thinking on the appropriate political reforms to support Africa's economic recovery. The large aid donors, the multilateral financial agencies, and, reluctantly or not, African governments now subscribe to the new consensus. A minimal liberal state, enabled by capacity-building initiatives and disciplined by a democratic politics, is efficiently and effectively to maintain the legal, administrative, political, and infrastructural conditions for private capital accumulation. Such a rejuvenated and reformed state will not only safeguard human rights, but also (it is believed) advance the developmental objective articulated on all sides – an environmentally sustainable and equitable pattern of growth. This is a bold, though problematical, vision.

The abiding faith in a minimal state is the first problematical aspect. This faith rests on a widespread disillusion with central governments in the 1980s. The public sector in industrialized democracies, communist countries, and the Third World alike had become a major, and often inefficient, consumer of resources. Many governments ran high budget deficits that appeared to contribute little to growth or welfare, while feeding inflationary pressures. In Africa in particular, scholars and outspoken citizens denounced governments for their rapacity, capriciousness, and wastefulness. Yet this anti-state reaction ignored a salient truth. The experience of industrializing countries suggests that underdeveloped countries will not achieve rapid development in the modern, highly competitive world without extensive governmental economic action. Hence, a policy aimed at severely reducing the economic role of African states, though it may be defensible in the short run, is not optimal in the longer term.

Alexander Gerschenkron's classic exploration of European

industrialization in the nineteenth century established the proposition that the greater a country's economic backwardness, the more its economy needed strong state intervention to overcome structural obstacles (Gerschenkron 1963). Britain, the trailblazer, could industrialize on the basis of private initiative and limited state action owing to the relatively simple nature of industrialization in the early eighteenth century. Not only did Britain have few competitors, but technology, being relatively simple, required limited capital and organizational resources. But later industrializers confronted changed circumstances. Competition was intense, and technologies were complex and large-scale, hence expensive. To mobilize the necessary human and capital resources required more extensive central coordination. Thus, when Russia undertook industrialization in the late nineteenth century, neither capitalists nor investment banks could supply the requisite finance capital. The Russian state had to play a direct financial role as a substitute for both.

This analysis can be extended to the economic challenge facing developing countries today. Those societies with state institutions able and willing to play an active economic role *of the right sort* – one that complements rather than replaces market forces – will be at a competitive advantage. The tasks of this developmental state extend far beyond the mere creation of an 'enabling environment' for private enterprise, the position adopted by the World Bank and others. The tasks must include, as well, one or usually more, of the following: to mobilize domestic and foreign savings, identify a potentially lucrative niche within the global market economy, orchestrate incentives to ensure that domestic firms play their assigned roles and have access to requisite factors of production, foster local mastery (not simply transfer) of modern technologies, and participate directly in strategic investments when high risks discourage private investors.

The 'secret' of the East Asian Newly Industrializing Countries, as is now widely recognized, is a strong, interventionist, yet market-conforming state. A noted authority on East Asia describes the intricate government–business relationship in Japan, South Korea, and Taiwan in these terms:

A developmental elite creates political stability over the long term, maintains sufficient equality in distribution to prevent class or sectoral exploitation (land reform is critical), sets national goals and standards that are internationally oriented and based on nonideological external referents, creates (or at least recognizes) a bureaucratic elite capable of administering the system, and insulates its bureaucrats from direct political influence so that they can manage technocratically.

'Managing technocratically' is a delicate and skill-intensive task:

The intent of the public system is to manipulate the inputs into the decision-making processes of privately owned and managed enterprises in order to achieve development goals, but the content of its inputs is continuously affected by feedback on profit-and-loss conditions, export prospects, raw materials costs, and tax receipts. The intent of the private system is to maximize profits, limit risks, and achieve stable growth given the political-economical environment in which it must operate, but its decisions on products, markets and investments are continuously affected by changing costs and availability of capital, export incentives, licensing requirements, and all the other things the government manipulates. (Johnson 1987: 141, 142)

Pace the World Bank, Africa does not need less government *per se*. Rather, Africa needs active, developmental states capable of complementing and directing market forces. There has, in the words of a prominent development economist, been 'a tendency for the reaction against *dirigisme* to go too far' (Killick 1989: 32). Different analysts pinpoint different tasks that African governments must undertake to foster economic recovery. One specialist observes that success in structural adjustment requires complex political-administrative interventions to ensure facilitative conditions at both the international and domestic levels (Callaghy 1989: 115–38). Governments must have the skill to negotiate successfully with the International Monetary Fund, the World Bank, and Western governments for flexible adjustment terms and generous inflows of resources. And, at the domestic level, political authorities must both insulate technocratic agencies charged with economic policy from societal pressures, and buffer organized groups, such as urban workers, from the full negative impact of demand-management. Another noted authority focuses upon declines in the savings and investment rates in sub-Saharan Africa between 1978 and 1988 as a major cause of the region's problems. These rates are now too low to support sustained economic growth. He therefore calls for developmental states which mobilize savings via 'an efficient, equitable and buoyant tax system'. He immediately notes, however, that this is 'not easy to achieve in current African conditions' (Helleiner 1990: 43).

In a sense, Africa in the 1980s suffered from too little government rather than too much. Governments, on paper, have been highly interventionist, overseeing a plethora of regulations, controls, services, and public investments. In practice, many governments were so lacking in authority, resources, and expertise that they have been unable even to control a burgeoning black market, smuggling, and simmering insurrections, let alone design and implement complex economic policies, maintain essential services, or engage in strategic planning. Hence, programmes to augment the efficacy (and responsiveness) of African states deserve a very high priority.

However, in light of the hostile historical, social, and material conditions reviewed in Chapter 2, the realist becomes a pessimist when forecasting whether institutionalized, effective, and predictable states will soon emerge in Tropical Africa. Developmental states capable of extensive economic direction are not an immediate prospect. Therefore, in the short run, African states must reduce their economic responsibilities to bring these responsibilities into balance with their currently limited capabilities. This entails the formation in the 1990s of 'liberal' states, whose economic task is to maintain a minimal enabling environment for the private sector. Retrenchment may also, as a beneficial by-product, curtail the deleterious 'winner-take-all' attitude toward politics; it may channel the energies of ambitious individuals away from an obsessive scramble for political influence, and towards productive entrepreneurial activities. In the longer term, far-sighted programmes of capacity-building may foster governments capable of assuming the expanded responsibilities of pro-active developmental states.

What are the policy implications of this strategy? Regimes proclaiming a commitment to 'reform', and encouraged by the international financial institutions, have sprung up all over Africa. What have these reformers achieved, what can they reasonably hope to achieve, and what dilemmas do they face, in retrenching governmental responsibilities and building institutional capacity?

It is not a simple matter to compress substantially a state's size and economic role. There are, first, limits to just how much the public sector can be reduced. The precariousness of public order counsels

Table 3. *Public employment reduction mechanisms for selected countries, 1981–1990*

Country	Ghost removal	Enforced/ early retirement	Voluntary departure	Retrenchment (regular staff)	Retrenchment (temporary staff)	Other mechanisms	Total[a]
Cameroon	5,830[b]	5,000	–	–	–	–	10,830
Central African Republic	2,950[b]	–	1,200	350–400	–	–	4,500–4,550
Congo	–	–	–	–	–	2,848[c]	2,848
The Gambia	–	–	–	919	2,871	–	3,790
Ghana	11,000[d]	4,235[e]	1,744	44,375[e]	–	–	48,610
Guinea	1,091[f]	10,236	1,960	–	–	25,793[g]	38,864
Guinea Bissau	800[d]	945	600	921	–	–	3,826
Mali	–	–	600	–	–	–	600
São Tomé and Príncipe	–	–	4	–	294[b]	–	298
Senegal	497	747	1,283	–	–	–	2,527
Uganda	20,000[i]	–	–	–	–	–	20,000

[a] Gross figures not adjusted for new recruitment and attrition.

[b] Elimination of ghosts and double payments.

[c] Attrition through hiring freeze.

[d] Refers only to ghosts identified. Their removal has not been verified in technical analysis.

[e] Includes staff in district assemblies and the education services.

[f] Ghosts in Guinea Conakry. A second census in 1989–90 identified a large number of additional ghosts.

[g] Of this figure, 10,810 officials were assigned to a personnel bank and placed on administrative leave, and 14,983 were removed from civil service rolls through parastatal liquidations and the transfer of employees of mining joint ventures to company rolls. Whether all of those placed on administrative leave have left the service or not remains unclear.

[h] An undetermined but small portion of these may be regular staff.

[i] Estimate based on savings from ghost removal exercise divided by average civil service wages.

Source: World Bank, *The Reform of Public Sector Management: Lessons from Experience*, Policy and Research series No. 18, Washington, DC, 1991, Table 2.1, p. 17.

against major reductions in the security and police forces. And even a liberal, market-oriented state needs a large cadre of civil servants to foster and maintain a supportive, enabling environment for entrepreneurs. Also, declaring civil servants redundant is a dangerous political proposition in countries where alternative employment prospects are negligible, and where budget deficits limit severance payments. Chapter 2 alluded to the dilemma that economic crisis places even greater pressure on the government to act as 'employer of last resort' than in more prosperous times.

In light of these considerations, the compression of the civil service achieved in some countries is quite remarkable (see Table 3). Governments have been encouraged by foreign donors to place a freeze on new hiring (except in certain key agencies or ministries), to close some of their embassies, ferret out 'ghost workers' from the employment roster, declare some excess workers redundant, and stringently control salary and benefits costs. The Central African Republic (CAR) managed to cut its civil servants' wages bill by about 2 billion CFA francs ($US7.5 million) by these methods in 1989–90 (*Africa Research Bulletin* 31 Mar. 1991: 9874). In Guinea-Bissau, a three-year structural adjustment programme which began in 1987 required extensive retrenchments in the public sector. Of a total of 16,000 government employees in this small West Africa country, 3,826 retired, quit, were struck off the payroll, or were laid off in 1988 and 1989. Neighbouring Guinea undertook an equally stringent retrenchment. One aim of its World Bank supported recovery programme in the late 1980s was to trim its bloated civil service from 90,300 to under 40,000 within several years. To ease the shock, the government encouraged early retirements, paid salaries for two years to those declared redundant, and sought to eliminate favouritism from the selection process. Nonetheless, discontent over rising prices and diminishing employment sparked riots in Conakry in 1989 (Topouzis 1989: 40–1).

Some governments have effected considerable savings just by eliminating 'ghost workers' from the salary rolls. In Sierra Leone, the IMF insisted in 1987 that the government reduce its salary bill. It managed to shave about 40 per cent off its salary payments by 1988–9 mainly by removing from its roster non-existent employees whose salaries were fraudulently collected by well-connected insiders. Relatively few real employees were actually sacked (Zack-Williams 1990: 26).

The Kenyan government has long been under pressure from donors to eliminate abundant overstaffing in its civil service. Its Sessional Paper No. 1 of 1986 on economic management and renewed growth acknowledged that the government could not continue to expand employment in the civil service at 7.4 per cent per annum, the rate of the previous decade. Yet little concrete action followed until 1990. The government's reluctance can probably be traced to its desire to dilute the Kikuyu preponderance in the public sector by recruiting employees from the smaller tribes, its power base. In 1990, the Moi government finally signed an agreement with its principal aid donors which required it to reduce employment and salaries in the civil service over two years. No longer would the government guarantee employment to all qualified graduates of universities and government training institutions. There would be no further recruitment or upgrading of positions without authorization from the Treasury. And salaries of teachers and civil servants were not to increase by more than 4 per cent per annum (below the rate of inflation). This plan met with outrage on the part of university students and others (*Weekly Review* 13 July 1990: 28–9).

In Ghana, 'redeployment' of public employees has a longer history than in most other sub-Saharan countries. The goal of this euphemistic exercise, which is to run from 1987 to 1998, is to eliminate overstaffing and create a younger, more efficient bureaucracy. Evidently, the civil service was bloated by nepotism and political favouritism in 1987. According to one investigator, '[i]n some departments you found three typists employed for one typewriter, ten drivers for only one vehicle. And you saw them sitting around all day doing nothing' (*West Africa* 14–20 Aug. 1989: 1325). The rate of 'redeployment' has been significant: a reduction of about 12,000 public employees in each of 1987 and 1988, and of about 14,000 in 1989 (World Bank 1991b: 20). The retrenchment strategy was carefully thought through to minimize the political outcry in the urban centres. The age of retirement was lowered to sixty years. Impartial Manpower Appraisal Committees were brought into the ministries to identify redundant employees. Those laid off received relatively generous severance pay and retraining or upgrading of their skills.

Nonetheless, the programme has been only a qualified success. Not only were some redeployed employees dissatisfied, but many civil servants felt demoralized and bitter (*West Africa* 14–20 Aug.

1989: 1326). Many thought favouritism and nepotism had played a role in selecting redundant employees, despite the Manpower Appraisal Committees. Many also were sceptical of the efficacy of the programme. They believed that the same pressures to overstaff the civil service would resurface – nepotism practised by top political and bureaucratic officials; bribes for jobs; and poor management.

These Ghanaian sceptics raised a point of broader relevance: the politicization of civil service recruitment and public management, once established, will prove difficult to reverse.

Privatization of public corporations is touted as a prime means to shrink the state's size and economic role, reduce fiscal deficits, and enhance economic efficiency. It is not, however, the panacea for overregulated economies that neo-conservatives portrayed it to be in the early 1980s.

Parastatals proliferated in post-colonial Africa for sound economic and social reasons. It is therefore not easy to dispense with them now, even if buyers can be found. Parastatals emerged or extended their sway as newly (and usually fleetingly) enfranchised electorates demanded the fruits of independence: jobs and services such as education and vocational training, health facilities, clean water, public transport, and housing. Business interests demanded improvements in electricity supplies, communications, transport, technical training, and credit facilities for budding urban and rural entrepreneurs. The weakness of domestic bourgeoisies prompted governments to fill the entrepreneurial void that would otherwise have been filled, if at all, by foreign capital. Nationalization of some foreign-owned companies, mainly those in the natural resource sector and commerce, and joint ventures with many others were an understandable nationalist response to extreme economic dependency. But the regular civil service was not equipped to act entrepreneurially or to assume new technical functions. And so existing parastatals expanded and new ones were created to provide social services, run public utilities, and manage or oversee commercial, financial, and productive activities.

Whatever the original rationale, most African parastatals have not fulfilled their promise. One comprehensive survey in the mid-1980s concluded that these public enterprises (PEs)

present a depressing picture of inefficiency, losses, budgetary burdens, poor products and services, and minimal accomplishment of the non-commercial objectives so frequently used to excuse their poor economic performance. Though every African country has one or more PEs which perform well by the most stringent of standards, on the whole, PE sectors are not fulfilling the goals set for them by African planners and leaders. (Nellis 1986: ix)

Fragmentary evidence bears out this harsh judgement. In Ghana, an independent study identified 181 enterprises in the early 1980s in which the government owned all or a majority of the shares, and 54 in which the government held a minority position. More than half of all these public enterprises made losses in the period 1979 to 1982. Total losses rose from 92 million cedis ($US13 million) in 1979 to 2.9 billion cedis ($US136 million)[1] in 1982 (*West Africa* 3–9 Sept. 1990: 2396). A study of the public sector in neighbouring Côte d'Ivoire tells a similar story. Between 1982 and 1985, 100-per cent owned public enterprises lost 85 billion CFA francs ($US175 million), while those which were 51–99 per cent state-owned lost 10 billion CFA francs ($US21 million). On the other hand, corporations with less than 50 per cent state ownership made a profit of 144 billion CFA francs ($US297 million) (*West Africa* 29 Oct.–4 Nov. 1990: 2748). The pages of *The Weekly Review* (Nairobi) are filled with reports of bungling by Kenya's public enterprises. A report of the Public Investment Committee of Kenya's National Assembly in 1990 documented massive losses by some of the country's 150 parastatals. It attributed this poor performance to mismanagement, inadequate budgetary control, overstaffing, and unaccountable and arrogant managers (*Weekly Review* 30 Nov. 1990: 36–7).

Some of the impediments to a sound performance by parastatals are generic, others are peculiar to Africa or underdeveloped countries. A generic problem is the ambiguous and even contradictory objectives that governments often assign them: how are public corporations to be profitable and also advance social goals such as employment generation, subsidized services or goods, and regional equalization? The fact that they are normally monopolies further impedes their performance by reducing incentives for efficiency. One problem peculiar to parastatals in Africa and other very poor countries is technical and managerial weaknesses, partly because the private sector (if it exists) attracts the ablest with higher salaries and superior career prospects. Another peculiar problem is the shortage of foreign exchange and shrinkage of public revenues stemming from the contemporary economic crisis. As a result, many African public utilities and state-owned enterprises have periodically or chronically been unable to import the necessary equipment, spare parts, and materials to operate efficiently.

As if all this were not enough, there is the pervasive problem of political interference. Parastatals, in principle autonomous from government in their day-to-day activities, are rarely tightly insulated from politics anywhere. However, in sub-Saharan Africa, the degree of political interference tends to be extreme by any standard. It is not unusual for political leaders improperly to intervene in parastatals to determine: 'who should be hired, who cannot be fired, where contracts must be awarded, who should receive credit, what bills should be paid and which can safely be ignored, and where services will be provided and maintained, despite insufficient revenues' (Nellis 1986: 36). These practices are a reflection of the clientelistic relations associated with neo-patrimonial governance, as discussed in Chapter 2. But irrespective of their political rationale, they undermine the technical rationality, and hence efficiency, of the affected parastatals.

In Nigeria, patronage and personal aggrandizement had sapped the competence and efficiency of public corporations as early as the 1960s. Consider the testimony of one official who has worked for several Nigerian statutory corporations over many years (Mbanefo 1975: 289–99): 'the strong grip of favouritism and "old-boys club" ties allows practically all the staff of these enterprises, who have control over the revenue generating sources of these enterprises, to grossly undercharge their friends and relations who use the services'. This accounts for a major loss of revenues. In addition, control of assets is so minimal in many public utilities that 'unscrupulous staff members have diverted assets ... to their private use without being found out'. The accounts of many public corporations can therefore not be reconciled. To make matters worse, inexperienced or incompetent political insiders are placed in top positions, including the office of general manager, for political reasons. '[T]hese organizations are ... over-staffed with redundant personnel who have no other reason for being there than they must be maintained by someone at the expense of one of these public enterprises.'

The World Bank, the International Monetary Fund, and bilateral donors have argued that these sorts of problems justify including privatization in structural adjustment programmes. The first target in countries which depend upon commodity exports is generally the state-owned marketing boards. So far, however, the scale of privatization has been modest. Nigeria has advanced rapidly, selling off 39 state-owned enterprises in 1989 and 29 in 1990, with a further 90 enterprises for sale in 1991. But many other governments are still largely in the planning stage. It is a complex business to value the assets of parastatals, unravel the complex legal problems involved in privatization (especially concerning responsibility for debts), and devise a regulatory framework for those corporations which will continue to operate as monopolies, though in private hands. Since many African governments lack the technical expertise to undertake this preparatory work, the World Bank and other agencies have provided technical assistance.

There are many other hurdles to successful privatization, besides these technical limitations. For one thing, the IMF/World Bank ideology may be flawed. A main tenet is that the indigenous private sector, once relieved of the dead hand of the state and provided with an appropriate enabling environment, will rise to the challenge. Entrepreneurs will appear to take advantage of new opportunities, and their dynamism will propel economies into broad-based growth. Structural adjustment policy focuses upon small enterprises. These are seen as both less dependent on tariffs and subsidies than large corporations, and more within reach of the managerial and entrepreneurial talents of local businessmen. Hence, since the mid-1980s, many governments have received assistance from the World Bank and other aid agencies to promote micro-enterprises. In Ghana, for example, a National Board for Small Scale Industries was created in 1985 to make credit available to small entrepreneurs.

But the success of the private-sector policy is not yet evident, even in Ghana which has pursued a market-oriented course since 1983. Local investors may hold back because they continue to mistrust governmental intentions or fear political instability. In Ghana, for example, entrepreneurs have apparently still not forgotten the scapegoating of traders and the harsh punishment meted out to those accused of economic crimes by the Rawlings government during its early populist phase. Also, Ghana's entrepreneurial ethic may have been smothered during the long period from 1960 to 1983, when a succession of governments assumed a parasitical or anti-capitalist economic orientation (with two short-lived, IMF-backed phases of economic liberalization). In any case, national bourgeoisies were always weak in most African countries; today, even with economic recovery programmes, business people remain constrained by such things as limited education, highly competitive markets owing to the liberalization of imports, poor infrastructure, a paucity of capital, and inadequate credit.

There is also a tendency for politicians and political insiders to resist reform or privatization of state-owned corporations, in the well-founded belief that this will diminish their sources of patronage as well as of bribes and kickbacks. In Zimbabwe, for instance, the government's reluctance to knuckle under to IMF/World Bank strictures on parastatal reform stems partly from political exigencies. 'Since parastatals have traditionally been used as a way to distribute patronage, both to individuals and to groups, it is ... exceptionally hard to either improve or eliminate them' (Herbst 1989: 81).[2] However, conditions now attached to loans and credits offer African governments limited options: they must either privatize public enterprises; 'commercialize' them by, if possible, subjecting them to competition, augmenting managerial autonomy, and reducing budgetary subsidies; or, if public enterprises continue to lose money, liquidate them.

Another hurdle is the frequent paucity of indigenous buyers eager to purchase state-owned enterprises. This problem arises owing to the absence or weakness of capital markets, and/or to the unprofitability of some indebted public enterprises in a depressed economy. Liquidation may be the most rational alternative in the case of some inefficient parastatals. Where unemployment and poverty are already major problems, however, this is an unpopular option. Governments are therefore tempted to sell parastatals to foreigners, even if the terms leave few benefits and significant costs to the host economy. Monopolies have continued in some sectors, though now the beneficiaries are foreigners rather than public corporations. And governments have agreed to assume the debts of parastatals sold to private concerns. This can be an expensive strategy: the Nigerian government learned in December 1989 that the debts of its state-owned enterprises, for most of which it would be responsible, totalled 23 billion naira ($US3 billion).

Togo's vaunted privatization programme seems to have provided excessive benefits to foreign purchasers. Eleven state-owned corporations were sold to private foreign companies in 1987–8. But, in some cases, the sale price only covered the severance pay of those employees made redundant as part of the purchase agreement. Also, the government had to assume the enterprises' outstanding debts in order to find foreign buyers. And some of the manufacturing parastatals, for example the Société Togolaise de Sidérugie steelworks and the textile mills sold to South Korean–American Pan African Textile Corporation, operate as virtual monopolies behind tariff walls – and with credit provided by the World Bank's International Finance Corporation and the African Development Bank (*West Africa* 28 Aug.–3 Sept. 1989: 1412). The question is: with more efficient management and the same concessions, could not these firms have made profits under public ownership? Some Togolese public corporations, such as the Société Nationale de Commerce, have made money under similar monopoly conditions.

The hurdle in other cases is not the absence of citizens willing and able to bid for state assets, but the absence of *politically acceptable* buyers (Nellis and Kikeri 1989: 668). If political leaders fear that privatization will augment the economic power of 'undesirable' ethnic or racial groups, they will delay the process or agree only to float small issues of the stock of designated parastatals. Kenya is a case in point. Although the government committed itself to privatization in the early 1980s, it stalled its implementation. By the end of 1990, the government had permitted only a minority of the shares of seven public enterprises to be sold to the public. Kenya's *Weekly Review* (14 Dec. 1990: 19), with unusual candour, explained the government's lackadaisical approach: 'privatisation of parastatals has the potential to exacerbate the existing racial and ethnic imbalances in the country, with regard to the ownership of wealth'. During the Kenyatta era (1962–78), Kikuyus disproportionately filled the top posts in the expanding number of parastatals. They used their influence and experience to gain bank credit and contracts to advance private businesses, and to secure lucrative positions in the boardrooms of transnational corporations. Following the attempted coup of 1982, President Moi dumped his Kikuyu lieutenants and began to move his allies among the Kalenjin and other smaller tribes into executive positions in the state apparatus. It was just at the point that the newly influential parastatal executives were converting their political influence into wealth in the private sector that the donors demanded privatization. To have acceded to this demand would not only have eliminated the political basis of accumulation on the part of Moi's allies, but also have shifted more economic power into the hands of the wealthy and seasoned Kikuyu and Asian businessmen. Since Moi found this politically unacceptable, he responded by endorsing privatization in principle while delaying the process in practice.

The Ghanaian case provides a vivid illustration of the range of problems bedeviling privatization in sub-Saharan Africa. Governments of differing political stripes had spawned well over 200 public corporations since independence: to create jobs, accelerate economic development, retain economic sovereignty, and fulfil social objectives (e.g., the State Fishing Corporation was supposed to make a cheap source of protein available to all Ghanaians). But most of them lost money. In 1986, the government devoted 8 per cent of its budget to the support of the state-owned enterprises. These enterprises were also allowed to fall into arrears on taxes and social security contributions, and on payments on government-guaranteed foreign loans. Poor management, corruption, embezzlement, and political interference accounted for this fiscal irresponsibility (Morna 1988: 61).

The travails of the State Fishing Corporation are indicative. It had eighteen managing directors between 1960 and 1988. Unstable and poor management has meant that fish have been sold illegally on the high seas at a great loss to the corporation, and that ships have been laid up owing to a lack of proper maintenance. A chronic shortage of spare parts spawned by the economic crisis has also played a part in the decrepitude of the corporation's ships. And the legal requirement that fish be sold at the same price everywhere in Ghana has cut into the corporation's earnings. The result was that only eight of the fleet of twenty-two vessels were seaworthy by 1988, and that fish delivered by the corporation declined from 38,000 tons in 1974 to only 2,400 tons in 1987. Not surprisingly, therefore, the State Fishing Corporation was among the thirty-two public enterprises slated for privatization in 1988.

Yet it has not been easy to find buyers. Ghana's state-owned enterprises were overstaffed by a total of 53,000 employees in 1988, according to a consultant (Morna 1988: 62). Only a few corporations offered the prospect of solid profits, such as the State Hotels Corporation and Tema Shipyards, but not the State Fishing Corporation. Also the indigenous private sector was still traumatized by the summary justice meted out to business people by the government of Flight-Lieutenant Jerry Rawlings, and limited by the absence in 1988 of capital markets on which to make large-scale public offers. Finally, trade liberalization had confronted indigenous industrialists with stiff competition from imports. Consequently, foreign investors snapped up a few lucrative public corporations, as has happened throughout sub-Saharan Africa. Other public corporations had to be retained or liquidated.

Privatization is thus fraught with difficulties and, if implemented, may not rejuvenate the private sector. After surveying the available evidence, two authorities conclude:

the significance of privatisation as a policy option for all LDCs has been greatly exaggerated. In some countries, denationalisation is likely to be difficult to achieve, its budgetary and economic benefits often appear to be limited, and it may involve significant political costs. Furthermore, the public enterprise sector is frequently used to meet distributional and other social objectives that would be sacrificed if the enterprises were transferred to private ownership. (Cook and Kirkpatrick 1988: 31)

Decentralization, in the form of devolution of powers and financial resources to elected local governments, is another core reform of the liberal-democratic programme. In principle, local government has much to recommend it. Top-down, bureaucratic management of development in Africa has rarely worked well. By relieving the overload and congestion in the central administration, devolution should enhance efficiency at all levels. It should also augment the responsiveness and accountability of government to local electors. Given the relative smallness and comprehensibility of local governments, their electorates are in a position to hold local political leaders directly accountable for their actions. And some argue that local participation in decision-making is not only a means to other ends, but an important goal in itself. It may ultimately allow the poor majority to increase their organizational strength, and hence their ability to advance their own interests.

But experiments in local empowerment in sub-Saharan Africa have seldom fulfilled their promise. Factional fights, poor performance in the delivery of services, and corruption have often sullied the repute of devolution. This divergence between the promise and the reality has predictably bred disillusion in central administrators and development agencies, and reinforced pressures toward centralization. Hence, a cyclical movement between centralization and decentralization has characterized the post-colonial history of many African countries.

Local government was fashionable in the first few years of independence, especially in the former British colonies. Colonial governments in the British-ruled territories had made an effort to extend local authorities into the rural as well as the urban areas. The French instituted only town governments. By independence most local councils were wholly or mainly composed of elected members. But a benevolent governmental attitude toward local autonomy soon vanished.

The poor performance of local authorities, local factional power struggles, and the prevailing *dirigiste* approach to development gave central governments a pretext to subordinate local governments. The latter, if they were not simply abolished outright (as in Sierra Leone and Tanzania, both in 1972), saw their functions, financial independence, and control of administrative personnel eroded. Ministries and agencies of the central government monopolized public revenues and important functions. Local authorities were usually left with inadequate revenues and responsibility for such minor tasks as collecting trash, clearing public latrines, supervising market places, and supplementing some central government services. Local governments in the cities have, of course, played a larger role, though usually under the supervision of the central government. Even capital cities suffered this erosion of independence and resources. Nairobi, for instance, was first denied a major source of independent revenue – the Graduated Personal Tax – in 1968, and then endured the withdrawal of all government grants in 1983. This placed the tax burden squarely on rate payers, many of whom predictably defaulted in their payments by the early 1980s. Direct administration of Nairobi through a board appointed by the central government in the 1980s failed to arrest the vicious circle of inadequate resources, demoralized and low-quality staff, poor and inadequate services, and a growing rate of tax default.

In the late 1970s or 1980s, it became manifest to both experts and citizens in various sub-Saharan countries that concentrating powers and responsibilities in the central government was not the solution. Popular disillusion with government grew along with the stagnation or decline of living standards, and with the evident inefficiency and corruption of remote and unaccountable bureaucracies. During this period, many governments experimented with deconcentrating administration to the district level (while retaining central control) and in creating or refurbishing the forms, though not the substance, of local government:

The result was ... a 'mixed' system of local administration: a means for seeking the public's support and identification with the State, employing structures of grassroots participation but not conceding real power to the local representatives. The 'deconcentrated' administrative officials retained control and responsibility for development activities; the representative local council where it existed was dominated by political and bureaucratic agents of the State system who possessed the bulk of information and consequently the power. (Mawhood 1987: 13)

The failure of this 'mixed' system had led by the late 1980s to a renewed interest in a real decentralization, that is, one involving a transfer of both powers and independent finances to local councils. This is the stage of the cycle we are now witnessing, with the ascendancy of the liberal-democratic, market-oriented programme. The key question is: can this cycle be broken, and the promised benefits of devolution be realized?

The continued vitality of local government in a few countries, such as Botswana and Zimbabwe, supports the notion that devolution can work effectively in Africa. In Zimbabwe, it is true, the central government has tightened its control over local authorities since the 1980 reform of the settler-dominated local government system. The Ministry of Local Government, Rural and Urban Development has supervised budgetary guidelines and the recruitment of the staff of the local councils, and it has replaced elected councils with appointed 'interim' administrations on several occasions. Although local governments must therefore act cautiously, they continue to provide important services in a relatively efficient manner (Wekwete 1988: 21).

Botswana boasts an unusually independent and effective system of local government. Since independence in 1966, the ruling Botswana Democratic Party has felt confident enough in its popularity to tolerate control of a few district and urban councils by opposition parties, and criticism of its policies by outspoken local councillors. The nine district councils and five urban authorities in this small Southern African country share powers at the local level with a competent and generally apolitical district administration, a tribal administration which mainly administers justice through customary courts, and land boards which allocate tribal lands in each of the main tribal areas. The councils are responsible for primary education, primary health care, ungazetted roads, water supplies, and trade and liquor licensing. They draw their recurrent revenues from a local government tax imposed on incomes. However, the local authorities are not without weaknesses. These include a shortage of qualified technical personnel, the low educational level of most elected councillors that restricts their understanding of technical issues, and the power of the central government to nominate a minority of local councillors, thus shifting the political balance in same cases (Tordoff 1998: 183–202; Picard 1987: 197). Despite these shortcomings, the Botswanan system has the distinction of providing decent and responsive government at local and national levels for a quarter-century.

Tanzania's experience, in contrast, illustrates the cycle of centralization and decentralization common in Africa, as first one and then the other alternative proved itself deficient. At independence in 1961, Tanzania inherited a local government system based on the British model. The government abolished these local authorities in 1972 on the grounds that they were ineffective in implementing governmental policies. In the place of local authorities, the government introduced a deconcentrated system of national planning controlled from the centre and a strengthened regional administration. This was an aspect of the centralization of power in the socialist one-party state.

But this strategy, too, foundered. Although the governing party managed to assert control over locally based opposition, this was at the expense of alienating local communities. Chama Cha Mapinduzi (CCM – the revolutionary party) could not, even if it wished to, coerce the people into support of its programmes. And it could not depend upon their voluntary mobilization unless the people played some role in selecting local leaders and influencing policies (Samoff 1989: 1–18). Hence, the government reintroduced elected local councils in 1984. They are responsible for local services, such as schools, local roads, and health services. A reintroduced poll tax (now called a 'development levy') financed local government, in conjunction with transfers from the central government.

This system, in turn, is deemed to have performed poorly (Jerve and Naustdalslid 1990: 1–2). People have resisted paying the development levy. They have continued to look to central government agencies to deal with their local problems. And corruption and inefficiency have become hallmarks of local councils. One of the main reasons for the malaise is the confusion in the role and functions of these councils *vis-à-vis* the central government and the governing party. Not only has the deconcentrated regional administration been retained, but the CCM organizationally parallels the state and local government structures ¬ and arrogates the right to guide policy at all levels. Reform of local government is on the horizon, as the government of President Ali Mwinyi canvasses opinion on the restructuring of government from top to bottom.

What are the prospects of success in the more recent experiments in devolution? To succeed, local governments will have to attract qualified and loyal staff, develop independent revenues, and shield themselves from the centralizing tendencies of national governments. The latter have justified their moves to control or replace local authorities by reference to the authorities' corruption, tribal divisions, factionalism, and inefficiency. However, this line of attack is more than mildly hypocritical. The main motive for central control is crassly political. Genuine devolution entails the rulers' loss of patronage, and the likelihood that political opponents will build local bases from which to challenge national leaders. Insecure ruling elites are therefore reluctant to cede staff, powers, and independent fiscal resources to local governments or communities. This being the case, most experiments in decentralization and local participation will abort as national authorities overtly reconsolidate central control.

Nigeria's programme to reform and rebuild local government as part of a phased transition to democratic government in 1992 may well fall victim to this political syndrome. Ironically, it has been the military governments (1966–79, 1983–92) that have favoured strong local government in this country. Civilian regimes (1960–6, 1979–83) have sought to subordinate local authorities to the federation's constituent states.

During the first military interregnum, a reform of local government laid the legal basis for a rejuvenated devolution of power. A decree in 1976 created 299 local government units with a list of exclusive powers over some local services and a list of concurrent powers with the state governments. The government guaranteed that these authorities would be adequately funded by assigning them the power to assess local rates and to receive statutory transfers from state treasuries. The councils were to be democratically elected. And state governments had designated supervisory powers over the actions of local governments within their jurisdictions. In practice, military governors in many states did not adhere to the spirit of these reforms: they continued to treat local governments as subordinate administrative units.

But the disdain for the institution of local government evinced by civilian state governors during the Second Republic (1979–83) was far worse. They flagrantly violated the constitution by using their regulatory powers to convert local governments into cogs in their political machines. '[M]ost governors dissolved elected local government councils as soon as they assumed office. In their place, they appointed management committees made up of party loyalists and other "clients"' (Osaghae 1989: 354). Local government councils were virtually 'local chapters of the ruling party in the state, and were governed strictly by the rules of the party hierarchy and discipline' (ibid.: 355). State governors also created new local authorities in order to expand the spoils of office; the number of local units rose from 301 in 1979 to 684 in 1982! And to make matters worse, many state governors refused to remit to the local councils their 10 per cent share of federal grants which they were constitutionally entitled to receive. Underfunded and poorly managed, local governments were soon crippled.

Local government reform is currently one element of President Babangida's carefully managed transition to democracy. In 1987, a military government again sought to buttress the autonomy and role of local councils as a means of checking the power of the states. Again, the central government assigned certain tasks and shares of federal transfer payments to local governments. And, following rowdy though generally fair non-party local elections in December 1987, elected councils again set out to assert their autonomy from military governors. Many conflicts have ensued. Only after President Babangida publicly upheld the importance of autonomous local government in his Independence Day speech in October 1988 did local councils free themselves from dependence on state governments for statutory grants.

The second set of local elections in December 1990 augured well for the future of local government in Nigeria. These were the first elections during the transition which involved a contest between the two officially recognized parties – the Social Democratic Party (SDP) and the National Republican Convention (NRC). Both parties cut across regional/ethnic/religious lines, though the NRC was associated in the popular mind with the conservative Muslim leadership of the Hausa–Fulani North (*African Guardian* 24 Dec. 1990: 28). Unusual for Nigeria, these elections were largely peaceful, free, and fair (ibid.: 28). Equally unexpectedly, the more progressive party, the SDP, emerged as the victor in terms of total councils captured.

But it is too soon to conclude that a revitalized and autonomous local government is firmly installed in Nigeria. Will the new civilian regime accept the independence and assertiveness now displayed by local elected councils? In light of Nigeria's history, this is unlikely. Insecure civilian state governors will probably once again subdue and subordinate local governments. The political insecurity of politicians 'gives little or no room for local will or initiative, no matter what the constitutional injunctions may be' (Osaghae 1989: 360). The status of local government will soon depend, once again, upon the grace of state governments.

The success of programmes to reform local government will depend upon meeting the political challenge that the Nigerian experience so graphically illustrates. The remedies are clear in principle, but difficult to attain in practice. A country's constitution will have to recognize the right of freely elected representative bodies to manage specified local affairs, and their exclusive control over particular financial resources. It will have to restrict a higher government's regulatory powers to ascertaining the conformity of local authority actions with legal requirements. In short, local governments must be able to defend themselves within an independent judicial system. Devolution is therefore indissolubly linked to the broader process of replacing personalistic or bureaucratic collectivist rule with an impersonal legal system.

Although central governments must reduce their responsibilities to a level commensurate with their limited capacities, such a reduction is difficult to achieve. Declaring civil servants redundant may not only heighten urban disaffection, but demoralize the remaining civil servants who believe that the process of selecting redundant employees is biased. Privatization will trim the tasks of the state by the transfer of state-owned enterprises wholly or partially into private hands. But indigenous entrepreneurs may not be able or willing to accept the challenge of turning public money-losers into private successes. And foreign investors may purchase public enterprises only on terms which are highly unfavourable to the host economy. Saddled with the accumulated debts of the privatized corporations and with various subsidies to the new owners, citizens may gain few if any benefits from the exercise. Finally, devolution of powers to local governments is an attractive way of curtailing the scope of the central government and enhancing efficiency, while broadening political participation. However, this enterprise, too, is fraught with difficulties, in particular the reluctance of central power-holders to acquiesce in the establishment of autonomous local councils.

Yet shrinking the state should be seen as only a short-term necessity. If, as argued above, a coherent, active, and effective state is a precondition of long-term recovery and development, then reform efforts must equally focus upon expanding state capacities. Some countries, such as Sudan, Somalia, Ethiopia, Uganda, Angola, Mozambique, Chad, Zaire, Liberia, and Equatorial Guinea, suffer a severe crisis of governability manifest in violence, instability, and an inability to implement public policy. Many of their neighbours exhibit less severe, though still onerous, problems of governability. Here the formation of coherent and disciplined states is a requisite for a civilized life free from political violence and the predatory exactions of public employees and private criminals. Institutional capacity-building is also a requirement for growth. Governments must be enabled to transcend the passive maintenance of an enabling environment to undertake the pro-active economic role which rapid development today demands.

Only recently have development agencies recognized the centrality of government to economic recovery. In the early 1980s debate focused on the pros and cons of particular liberal economic policies. Economists soon realized, however, that structural adjustment loans would only be used effectively if recipient governments possessed a modicum of institutional will and capacity. The World Bank signalled its concern in 1983 by devoting half of its *World Development Report* to public-sector management. By the late 1980s it was supporting programmes to improve public management in more than thirty sub-Saharan countries (Adamolekun 1989: 84). The Bank and its consultants advised African governments on reforms in two areas. One was civil-service management, including reduction or control of public employment, training, and reviews of salaries and compensation policy; the other was economic and financial management. In 1989, with the publication of *Sub-Saharan Africa: From Crisis to Sustainable Growth*, 'governance' (as it now was termed) moved to the forefront of the development agenda. The Bank's *World Development Report 1991* confirmed this priority; it concentrated on how market and state can pull together to revitalize development.

Yet the development agencies have favoured an unduly narrow approach to building state capacities. Consider the 'African Capacity Building Initiative' proposed by the World Bank, the African Development Bank, and the United Nations Development Programme in March 1990 (World Bank 1990b). It assumes that, in the area of institutional development, Africa's most important need is to augment the governments' capacity in policy analysis and economic management. The initiative thus aims to foster a critical mass of highly qualified African economic managers and policy analysts, and to ensure that these professionals can function effectively. These goals are to be achieved by rehabilitating departments of economics and public administration in African universities; providing scholarships for advanced study to African specialists; improving in-service training; reinforcing policy analysis units in key economic ministries; strengthening local consulting firms; and fostering five regional 'think-tanks' to train policy analysts and economic managers and undertake research on economic issues. Pledges for $100 million were procured from aid donors in 1991 to support this initiative.

One questions the adequacy, however, of an initiative that seeks to improve the analytical and management capacity of only economic agencies, such as planning bodies, finance ministries, and central banks. First, economic management and policy units cannot succeed as favoured enclaves within a generally decrepit state. Is it realistic to expect highly-trained technocrats to increase their leverage over economic policy design and implementation in state structures still dominated by personalistic-clientelistic practices? Are technocratic criteria likely to govern resource allocations in these circumstances? It is important to improve policy analysis and the management of economic agencies; it is equally important to improve the managerial capacity and discipline of the agencies that will implement the economic policies, for example, ministries of agriculture, education, and health. Secondly, a capacity-building initiative must address such complementary policy issues as recruitment to the civil service, salary structures, and terms of service, if it is to reverse the current inefficiency and malaise in African bureaucracies (Moharir 1990: 111).

State capacity-building is a complex and multifaceted process. Chapter 2 argued that rational, predictable, and effective economic management will prevail only if governments dispose of fiscal resources commensurate to their tasks, direct cohesive, specialized and competent bureaucracies, and command popular support which is not largely dependent upon clientelistic relationships. That chapter also explored the chief impediments to building effective states in sub-Saharan Africa. What can be done now to remove or at least alleviate these impediments?

Consider first the quandaries surrounding fiscal reform. Sierra Leone illustrates just how desperate the fiscal situation can become. Its finance minister noted in March 1990 that government spending in the first six months of the fiscal year on fictitious contracts, procurement of unbudgeted goods, over-pricing of goods purchased by the public sector, payments for goods that were not delivered, and excessive overseas travel accounted for 65 per cent of planned expenditure for the entire year. The Central Bank consequently had to print money equivalent to 20 per cent of the money stock at the outset of the year in order to finance the overspending. This predictably led to a rise in the already high inflation rate (*West Africa* 12–18 Mar. 1990: 408). Later, the finance ministry announced that tax evasion was equivalent to about 24 per cent of budgeted revenue. To increase revenues, the government would pay bonuses to all revenue-collecting agencies (including the police) which collected revenues above their targeted level (*West Africa* 25 Feb.–3 Mar. 1991: 268). Sierra Leone is admittedly an extreme case; but the fiscal position of many other sub-Saharan governments is not much better.

Emergency measures designed to cut fiscal deficits have frequently had counterproductive results.[3] Recall the problems identified in Chapter 2. First, governments have allowed high rates of inflation to erode the real wages of civil servants. This has lowered the salary bill, but at the expense of undercutting the incentive of civil servants to remain in their jobs or engage in sustained work. Secondly, governments have belatedly, and usually under external pressure, reduced public employment. However, these programmes have proven unpopular (unless only 'ghost workers' were terminated), undermining further the urban support for government. Thirdly, budgets have registered deep and usually indiscriminate cutbacks in capital and maintenance expenditures. Rapid deterioration of roads, electricity and water supplies, telecommunications, and educational and health facilities have unfortunately followed, along with productivity declines. Fourthly, delays by state agencies in payments of salaries and utility charges have temporarily lessened financial drains, but at the expense of further demoralization of civil servants and financial shortfalls in utility parastatals.

Finally, governments have introduced emergency taxes, such as surcharges on income taxes, 'solidarity taxes', 'development levies', luxury taxes, and higher excise duties on petrol, cigarettes, and beer. These measures, taken in conjunction with the other cutbacks and hardships, have been highly unpopular. They have sometimes sparked extensive urban riots and demonstrations. In Côte d'Ivoire, two months of sometimes violent strikes and street demonstrations in 1990 forced the government to abandon its plans for public-sector wage cuts and higher taxes. Instead, it undertook to improve revenue collection, combat smuggling, sell 4,000 state-owned vehicles, close some diplomatic missions, and reduce ministerial staff. The Gabonese government also moved in mid-1990 to mollify its aroused urban populace by abolishing various 'solidarity taxes' and other exactions.

These measures are, at best, only a temporary response to fiscal crisis. Although they generate some short-term relief, they alienate civil servants and the urban population, lower production, encourage capital flight, and discourage foreign direct investment as investors count the costs and uncertainties of deteriorating infrastructure and plummeting governmental popularity. Is there a longer-term and more benign approach to building an adequate fiscal basis for African states?

On the side of expenditure reductions, experts agree on some fairly obvious guidelines (Tanzi 1990: 29–32):

There should be no further savings from squeezing the real wages of civil servants. Instead, the emphasis should lie on shrinking public employment

by means of privatization of state corporations and retrenchment of redundant employees. Governments should not scrimp on the maintenance
of the infrastructure; they should, rather, scrutinize all proposed capital
expenditure to ensure that only those with high rates of return proceed.

Governments should reassess all existing state subsidies on the basis
that only those which assist the poorest or promote important social
objectives (such as urban mass transit) should continue. Public revenues
should not subsidize inefficient enterprises or the consumption of the
middle class.

Secure regimes should brave the displeasure of their officer corps by
cutting inflated military expenditures. The military budgets of most African countries are out of all proportion to the minimal threat of foreign
aggression.

While these policies make good financial sense, they are subject to a
familiar political constraint: the opposition of powerful vested
interests. Removing subsidies, retrenching civil servants, and
attacking the perquisites of the military will require careful planning
and exceptional government fortitude.

Tax reform poses equally knotty political problems. An effective
programme must satisfy three criteria (Shalizi and Squire 1988:
13–19):

Given yawning budgetary deficits and heavy external debts, tax reform
must not decrease total revenues.

Yet the contribution of export taxes and import duties to total revenues
must decline. This contribution exceeded 40 per cent in many sub-Saharan
countries in the mid-1980s. High taxes on commodity exports penalize
producers, thus discouraging production. High import duties may shelter
inefficient domestic manufacturers (though high duties on luxury imports
are warranted on equity grounds). Thus, the tax burden should be shifted
from production to consumption and income taxes.

Any contemplated reforms must be administratively feasible. They must
appear equitable, to limit tax evasion. And new tax regulations should not
be so complex, or so difficult to enforce, that they exceed the limited
capacity and discipline of tax administrations.

Specific reforms flow from these guidelines. Personal and corporate income taxes, which generated on average under 30 per cent of
total revenues in sub-Saharan countries in the early 1980s (Shalizi
and Squire 1988: 13), must increase their share. Tax experts agree
that this can most effectively be achieved by lowering the top rate

while eliminating many deductions from taxable income, and deducting taxes at source. Also, taxes on domestic consumption must rise as taxes on international trade decline. Equity considerations dictate that consumer necessities be exempted from increases in excise and sales taxes; increases would lower the demand from products which are often locally produced, and diminish further the living standards of the poor majority. The cost of some public services should also rise by introducing or raising user charges. (Even simply clearing up arrears in utility charges would help where, as in Kenya, governmental agencies, public corporations, and municipalities rarely pay their utility bills.) If charges are introduced or raised for services mainly consumed by industry and the well-off – such as sewerage, electricity, telecommunications, roads, and university education – then the reforms can be defended on the grounds of equity. Charges for basic health services or primary education are another matter. Value Added Tax is another widely discussed option, though transactions in the vast parallel economies would escape the taxman. Increases in excise taxes on alcohol, cigarettes, and petrol constitute another acceptable means of raising revenues – people grudgingly view them as equitable and inevitable.

But, if tax administration remains lax and corrupt, these reforms will not ease the fiscal crisis. Tax evasion is the rule rather than the exception in many underdeveloped countries (Khalilzedeh-Shirazi and Shah 1991: 45). The dimensions of the phenomenon are startling. In Burkina Faso, tax arrears at the end of 1989 amounted to two-thirds of budgetary receipts (*Africa Research Bulletin* 15 Nov.–16 Dec. 1990: 10189). In Ghana, collection of income and property taxes fell from 68.5 per cent of the expected total in 1988 to 17.3 per cent in 1989 (ibid. 28 Feb. 1990: 9836). In Nigeria, an investigation revealed that the treasury lost 24 million naira ($US3 million) in 1990 as a result of a single customs swindle involving importers and customs officers. The sophisticated scam used bogus cheques and bank drafts forged with the use of computers and printing machines (*West Africa* 4–10 Feb. 1991: 150–1).

Consider also user charges. It makes good sense, for instance, to raise utility charges to middle-class consumers – until one recalls the corruption and inefficiency that plague utility parastatals. One authority lists the main problems as 'theft of supplies, non-payment of bills, bribery of meter readers, falsification of contracts for investment and maintenance activities, misappropriation of funds, and a lack of good records and verifiable auditing procedures' (Anderson 1989: 535). Raising utility charges in this environment may merely induce customers to bribe utility employees to avoid higher bills. Revenues may even fall and services deteriorate further after user charges are introduced or raised, as corruption intensifies (ibid.: 535).

It is thus true that 'comprehensive rehabilitation of tax administrations must precede or at least accompany any major tax reform' (Shalizi and Squire 1988: 19). But how is this to be done?

Fiscal reform constitutes an enormous challenge in the context of a downward spiral of economic and political decay. It will require governments of exceptional integrity which are willing to avoid 'quick fixes' in favour of carefully planned, long-term programmes of tax reform, expenditure reductions, and rehabilitation of revenue collection agencies. The financial guidelines for these programmes are clear; the political and administrative implications are wide-ranging and onerous.

Upgrading administrative capacity represents another uphill battle. The limited capability of state employees to identify problems, formulate policy alternatives, and implement policies will constrain economic development. Low pay and poor working conditions in many countries have lowered the productivity of civil servants, and driven some of the best and the brightest into emigration or private employment. Rampant clientelism has often vitiated the meritocratic principle and protected the incompetent or corrupt bureaucrat from retribution. Corruption has created bottlenecks in the processing of essential licences or approvals, and has induced people to regard public servants with contempt. Regulations are often arbitrarily administered.

Genuine reform of the bureaucratic apparatus will normally require more than just tinkering with existing structures and processes. A major task will be to expand, upgrade, and motivate the trained professionals and support staff in the civil service and public corporations. Tight budgets in the 1980s generally impelled a decline in the quality of education from primary school through post-secondary educational institutions. Now that trend must be reversed, if countries are to have an adequate supply of educated personnel to fill key positions in the public and private sectors. The

World Bank's seminal report of 1989 (1989a) recognized this exigency in stressing that Africa's economic recovery depended heavily upon the development of human resources and institutional capacity. The report therefore proposed that African governments double the resources devoted to human resource programmes – to 8 or 10 per cent of GNP. It also expected donors to subsidize recurrent as well as capital expenditures in advanced educational institutions.

If sufficient numbers of skilled professionals and technicians are trained, how is the civil service to attract, retain, and motivate them to make their best effort? Salaries in the public sector must certainly be substantially increased in countries where they have deteriorated to abysmal levels. Only then will highly qualified personnel make their careers in the civil service, and spend their time on the job rather than on private income-earning ventures. Botswana, whose civil service is highly regarded for its competence and effectiveness, is one of the few sub-Saharan countries whose public salaries have not fallen behind the rate of inflation. It is this country's unusually high rate of economic growth that has underwritten these generous salary scales.

But how can other countries improve significantly the salaries of their civil servants? Heavily indebted governments do not have the revenues. Even if they do, conditions attached to their structural adjustment loans place restraints on public expenditure. Although many governments have revised salary scales upwards, the real value of civil servants' salaries is still well below the level of a decade or more ago. Should the World Bank and other donors then supplement the salaries of professionals in public sectors, as some have proposed? This practice started in the 1980s as donors sought to attract and retain higher-level staff on donor-funded projects. Where the salaries of civil servants had been severely eroded, as in Ghana, Guinea-Bissau, Mozambique, Niger, and Uganda, donors felt they had no other option (World Bank 1991b: 21). But the experience has been judged a negative one: 'it defeats deeper, structural pay reform, and it tends to create an artificial alternative labor market in which wage levels can escalate out of control' (ibid.: 17). This demoralizes regular civil servants, and embarrasses host governments. Solutions to the salary conundrum remain elusive (Corkery and Bossuyt 1990: 18).

Salaries are not the only obstacle to retaining and motivating qualified civil servants. Top civil servants also need an appropriate intellectual and political environment, one which is conducive to open discussion of policy alternatives and even-handed implementation. In such an environment, politicians and civil servants will be held accountable for their actions, political interference in day-to-day administration and recruitment will be minimal, and top bureaucrats will be free to express their expert views on policy issues to their superiors. But ruling elites who have built their power on the basis of personalistic and clientelistic relations are unlikely to embrace reforms that replace their clients with apolitical technocrats. Realistically, administrative reform must not aim for the complete replacement of clientelistic criteria with technocratic ones. Such a transformation will be unlikely to succeed in poor and unintegrated societies. State bureaucracies will inevitably continue to some extent as employers of last resort. And this is not necessarily a bad thing, so long as clientelism retains only a secondary influence upon recruitment and resource allocation.

Finally, enabling states entails augmenting their political capacity, where this is weak. To act effectively, a state must not only control adequate resources and enable skilled technocrats to design and implement policies. It must also be able to count upon the spontaneous acceptance of the law by a majority of its citizens. Few African governments, however, appear to have rested on such consent. Citizens are understandably cynical; they have seen (or heard) how privileged individuals and groups have enriched themselves and evaded the law by means of bribery or collusion with state officials, and how insiders have used even the judicial system against their opponents. People thus feel justified in disregarding governmental edicts when they see them as contrary to their own interests. Compliance then comes to depend on patronage or force – both of which are in short supply. (Indeed, the externally prescribed shrinking of the public sector and public subsidies will progressively undercut the clientelistic basis of regimes.) In these circumstances, governments often lack the strength to implement reforms which entail sacrifices on the part of strategic groups, such as urban workers or professionals.

Political capacity therefore requires dramatic changes at two levels. The first is the ascendancy of a reformist regime which inspires trust because it breaks with the corrupt and despotic practices of the past. The second is a shift from mercenary pay-offs and force to consent as the primary basis of government. In principle, constitutionally enshrined human rights and democratization – core elements of the official consensus on the politics of Africa's recovery – should form a firm basis of consent and an antidote to undisciplined state behaviour. But will this political programme work as planned? This is the question to which we must now turn.

§ 4 §

DEMOCRATIZING LIBERAL
STATES

To arrest Africa's economic decline, the new consensus prescribes *glasnost* as well as *perestroika*. Political democracy and free markets are the twin panaceas. Democracy will serve to keep the liberal state honest and attuned to the societal interest in economic prosperity. Market forces will stimulate the entrepreneurial drives and productive energies that the dead hand of the monopolistic state has smothered or misdirected. The two goals are seen as indissolubly linked.

Realpolitik has doubtless played a part in facilitating the democratic tendency of the new consensus. With the waning of the Cold War, geopolitical considerations are no longer as compelling as formerly in the capitals of the major global powers. France, the United States, and Russia are no longer willing to support 'their' African strongmen against all challenges. Western liberal democracies and the international institutions they dominate are therefore now freer to pursue their natural preference for electoral democracies. Also, the widespread popular protests of the 1980s against authoritarian regimes in Eastern Europe, Latin America, and Africa would have encouraged Western regimes to claim paternity of the triumphant democratic tendency.

This new-found enthusiasm for democracy, though welcome, is problematical in two respects. Can liberal democracies emerge and survive in Africa? And, if so, will they indeed promote the equitable and sustainable growth that all commentators espouse?

The unpalatable reality is that sub-Saharan Africa is unlikely soon to yield many stable democracies. Just as the cultural, historical, political, and socio-economic conditions in Africa have not been fertile ground for nourishing strong, developmental states, they are generally unfavourable to democracy.

Yet the situation is far from hopeless. Although liberal democracies are still rare in Africa, their number is rapidly growing. These democratic experiments, though partial and fragile, are not doomed to failure. Cultural and socio-economic conditions vary significantly from one African country to the next. Historical circumstances in some countries have fostered a propitious popular mobilization against autocratic government. External pressures, in particular the ascendant liberal-democratic ideology now advocated by aid-donors, reinforce the influence of Africa's democratic proponents. And most political leaders will abandon authoritarian structures and adopt democratic reforms, if the long-run costs of delay seem ominously to outweigh the short-term benefits.

African political democracies are a recent phenomenon. If a stable liberal democracy is defined as a multiparty constitutional system that has survived for a decade or more, then Tropical Africa boasts only five cases among its forty-seven countries: Gambia, Senegal, Botswana, Mauritius, and Zimbabwe. The future of Zimbabwe is still uncertain as the country is led by a president, Robert Mugabe, who espouses the virtues of a one-party state.[1]

Madagascar might be considered a sixth case. It developed a hybrid system in the 1970s and 1980s, with elements of both a single-party and a multi-party system. Madagascar's first president, Philibert Tsiranana, was compelled by an urban rebellion to turn over power to the military in 1972. Since 1976, the Avant-garde de la Révolution Malagache (AREMA) under President Didier Ratsiraka has held power. Opposition parties have been allowed to run candidates in periodic legislative elections, but only if the parties were ideologically congenial to socialist AREMA and hence belonged to a loose coalition, the Front Nationale pour la Défense de la Révolution. Although the government censored all independent newspapers, and banned criticism of the president or the 'socialist revolution', human-rights abuses were rare. Nonetheless, this guided democracy failed to satisfy a large segment of the urban population: three months of street demonstrations orchestrated by a united opposition in mid-1991 forced President Ratsiraka to open up the political system.

Several other countries made transitions to multiparty electoral systems between 1989 and 1992. Namibia is widely praised for its democratic constitution and vigorous political life. It is too early, however, to judge the viability of political democracy in a country which acceded to independence only in 1989. Côte d'Ivoire and Gabon held multiparty elections in 1990 in which the governing party held on to power; but the opposition parties and foreign observers have alleged that electoral malpractices influenced the outcome. The two tiny island countries of Cape Verde and São Tomé and Principe were the first in the democratic wave of 1991 to see opposition candidates displace incumbent governments in free elections. Mauritius, an Indian Ocean country, was the only sub-Saharan case in which this had previously happened. When Nicephore Soglo defeated Benin's President Mathieu Kérékou in March 1991, Benin became the first mainland African country to vote its president out of office. Zambia followed, with the ouster of President Kenneth Kaunda and his party in October 1991. Nigeria, guided by a tough military regime, is in the midst of a lengthy democratic transition which reached the stage of two-party electoral contests at the local level in December 1990.

Critics have questioned the democratic credentials and stability of even the longer-established multiparty cases. An attempted coup in 1981 against the Gambian government of Sir Dawda Jawara was only defeated by the intervention of Senegalese troops and the declaration of a State of Emergency. The same government announced the foiling of another plot in 1988. Botswana has held six comparatively fraud-free national elections since 1965; however, all the major mass media are government owned, and occasional prosecutions and tape-recording of opposition politicians aim to intimidate opponents. When faced with growing urban support for opposition parties in the late 1980s, some leading officials of the ruling Botswana Democratic Party called for the creation of a one-party state. This renewed suspicions that the government would tolerate the opposition only so long as it represented no threat. In Mauritius, political stability is threatened by a resurgence of communal suspicions. The opposition coalition in the 1987 election campaign increased its support dramatically by playing upon Hindu caste divisions.

Senegal, which returned to a limited form of electoral democracy in 1976, saw its 1988 general election marred by fraud and political violence. President Abdou Diouf's Parti Socialiste expected this election to be merely a formality. But the campaign revealed a groundswell of urban support for the main opposition leader, Abdoulaye Wade. Nonetheless, the official results on 28 February awarded about 75 per cent of the vote to Diouf. Charging electoral irregularities (charges supported by journalists on the scene), opposition elements rioted in Dakar. The government then detained the principal opposition leaders and briefly arrested about 200 rioters under a State of Emergency. The exercise badly tarnished Senegal's image as a pluralistic democracy (Diop and Diouf 1990).

In Zimbabwe, human-rights organizations faulted the ZANU-PF government in the mid-1980s for its brutal suppression of an insurrection centred in Matabeleland, and for its use of emergency powers to harass the opposition Zimbabwe African People's Union. Ironically, the regime employed the security apparatus and laws inherited from the repressive white-settler government of Ian Smith. Tensions eased after December 1987, when ZAPU and ZANU-PF agreed to amalgamate under the banner of the latter. The State of Emergency, originally invoked by the Rhodesian Front government to squash ZANU and ZAPU, was lifted in 1990. Zimbabwe, since its national elections in 1989, would be classified as a one-party dominant system. ZANU-PF overshadows but tolerates the small and vociferous Zimbabwe Unity Movement opposition.

Even in the remaining one-party and military-controlled states, promises of political liberalization are the rule rather than the exception. Governments in the following countries have scheduled multi-party elections in 1992 or 1993: Angola, Cameroon, Chad, Congo, Guinea-Bissau, Kenya, Lesotho, Mali, Mauritania, Mozambique, Niger, Nigeria, Sierra Leone, Somalia, Tanzania, Togo, and Zaire. Uganda mounted elections for its National Resistance Council (parliament) in February 1989, albeit under regulations which banned parties and campaigning and required the queuing method for selecting representatives. Its president, Yoweri Museveni, has proclaimed that a democratic constitution, originally promised in 1990, will appear by 1994. Several regimes have taken steps to devolve powers and resources to elected local governments. Tanzania in 1984 partially reversed its earlier centralization policy; Uganda under the victorious National Resistance Movement established a nation-wide system of elected Resistance Councils in 1986; Nigeria held local elections in 1988 and 1990, and state elections in 1991, as part of its phased return to democracy; and Ghana in 1989 initiated a non-party district council system. And many tough-minded governments, such as those in Nigeria, Tanzania, Uganda, and

Kenya, have permitted independent magazines and newspapers some latitude in political criticism.[2]

Despite these promising signs, reforms still must overcome many obstacles. Africa's hostile conditions encumber not so much *transitions* to democracy as the *consolidation* of enduring democracies. The transition from authoritarian to democratic regimes involves the following formal changes:

1   the official recognition of civil and political rights;
2   the legalization of opposition parties and of their right to organize support;
3   the organization of interest groups to protect their own interests, including those which were previously controlled or repressed;
4   the constitutional enshrinement of a set of democratic institutions and procedures, including laws governing elections, the relationship between the executive and legislative powers, the independence of the judiciary, the role of local government, and so on.

Democratic consolidation, on the other hand, is a longer-term and less visible process. It involves strengthening the organizational coherence, autonomy, and popular support of institutions which adjudicate or publicize abuse of power, punish those who break the democratic rules, and disperse political power: the judiciary, local government, the party system, the press, the universities, and civil associations of various sorts.

Several of these key institutions belong to civil society, or link civil society to the state. Without a civil society willing and able to resist authoritarianism, democratic transitions may only be cosmetic, designed mainly for foreign consumption, or cyclical (as in Latin America), with democratic tendencies reversed by *coups d'état*.

One impediment to efforts to install and consolidate democratic systems is the lack of a unifying and facilitative political culture. Most favourable is the highly improbable situation in which both precolonial and colonial political traditions were in some measure compatible with democratic norms.

Few now accept the romantic view of the early 'African socialists' that traditional African societies were inherently consensual and democratic. Senegal's Léopold Senghor and Tanzania's Julius Nyerere, two of the more illustrious proponents of this view, argued that the competitive party system is inappropriate for African conditions. Political parties, Senghor maintained, represent social classes; but in Africa class divisions had not yet solidified, and could be forestalled. Nyerere contended that a multiparty system was both unnecessary and ethnically divisive. Political decision-making in Tanzania's traditional societies had involved community participation in discussions from which a consensus would emerge. A one-party democracy would build on this tradition by emphasizing unity, equality, and consensus (Nursey-Bray 1983).

Though compelling, these benign views have been discredited by the oppressiveness, inefficiency, and corruption of one-party states, and by the evidence of enormous variations in the political traditions of precolonial societies. Chapter 2 sketched the tendency of one-party states in Africa to suffocate civil society by regulating, coopting, or undermining intermediary institutions and controlling productive assets. Even Julius Nyerere has demanded that defenders of the single-party system in Tanzania furnish cogent reasons for its survival. Since the ruling party (CCM) was 'sleeping', he claimed, opening up the system to opposition parties might revitalize grassroots politics (*Daily News* [Dar es Salaam] 27 June 1990).

How compatible are traditional political values and institutions, on the one hand, and the modern democratic ones, on the other? One survey by a Kenyan historian of precolonial politics in East, Central, and West Africa sceptically concludes:

In Black Africa, whether the political system was that of the highly centralized states or of the amorphous non-centralized communities, it did not belong to a democratic tradition. There were rudiments of democratic principles and practices, especially in the non-centralized communities, but it would be dangerous to equate those practices with advanced forms of democracy ... (Simiyu 1987)

A British historian supports this general view (Lonsdale 1989); he contends that the consensual models of African chieftaincy were largely a myth perpetuated by colonial officials who wished to justify their alliances with the traditional rulers. Some nationalist leaders found this myth congenial, as it furnished a traditional basis for their single-party rule and/or African socialism. In reality, however, precolonial political practices were diverse and ambiguous. On the one hand, the factional politics of clientage widely held sway, and conflicts between centre and periphery abounded. On the other hand, rituals which vested the rulers with power usually also provided some mechanism for shielding their subjects from abuse of that power (Lonsdale 1989: 134). Even in the highly hierarchical empires of ancient Mali and Gao, people possessed channels through which to voice dissent (Ki-Zerbo 1986). However, mechanisms to discourage despotism are not equivalent to institutions for democratic decision-making.

Diversity is key. In Zaire, for instance, the paternalistic political cultures of precolonial societies laid the ideological foundations for President Mobutu Sese-Seko's authoritarian rule, rather than democracy. The familial idiom prevailed throughout the territory that now constitutes Zaire:

People regularly used the idiom of kinship both in the politics of small scale societies in the forest and in the Lunda empire in the southern savanna. In this latter case, people extended notions of kinship to refer to fixed political relationships ... in the Lunda state so that the holder of a hierarchically superior office became, in effect, a 'father' in relation to his 'sons', who held subordinate positions. (Schatzberg 1988: 83)

Belgian colonialists, including the Catholic hierarchy and the mining corporations, employed and deepened this culturally sanctioned paternalism to fortify their authority. Since 1965, Mobutu and his coterie have regularly utilized familial imagery to legitimate autocracy. For instance, the regime portrays 'those with enough temerity to protest, or even revolt ... as misguided children. Similarly, the metaphors enable Mobutu and those in power to portray political repression as firm "parental" discipline for prodigal "children" in need of a political spanking for their own good' (Schatzberg 1988: 91).

Nigeria, Africa's most populous country, illustrates the variation in political traditions even within a single country (Diamond 1988a: ch. 2). The three largest of Nigeria's 250 ethnic groups – the Hausa-Fulani, the Yoruba, and the Igbo – had vastly different political values and institutions. The Hausa-Fulani of the north, along with neighbouring groups such as the Nupe and Kanuri, trace their roots to autocratic, centralized, and bureaucratic precolonial states presiding over steeply stratified societies. The Yoruba in the west organized themselves in a loose confederacy of centralized and hierarchical kingdoms. Their monarchs, or *obas*, were elected by chiefs representing the non-royal lineages, and had to share some legislative and judicial powers with a council of chiefs that had the power to unseat a tyrannical ruler. The Igbo, in contrast to both, formed a plethora of acephalous and egalitarian societies with no sense of corporate identity before the twentieth century. Adult males had the right to participate in decision-making at the village level. The difference in scale between the Igbo village and the multiethnic Nigerian federal state, however, renders this democratic element of limited applicability to contemporary democratic experiments.

This historical setting does not conduce to the growth of a shared, democratic culture. Democratic activists enjoy, especially in the north, no tradition of tolerance of opposition, or freedoms of association and expression. Although negotiation and compromise were features of precolonial policies in the south, they were alien to the northern emirates. The only political tradition common to these three ethnic groups, and the remainder, is that of colonialism – and even that dates only from the unification of the north and south in 1914. Colonial rule was autocratic, bureaucratic, and centralized until a few years before independence in 1960. Still, despite this unpropitious cultural background, Nigerians have periodically demonstrated a striking attachment to political freedom since internal self-government in the 1950s.

Although the colonial heritage was principally autocratic, centralized, and paternalistic rule, in rare cases the indigenous elite did gain experience in, and commitment to, democratic procedures. For India, explanations of the survival of democracy point to the long history of party organization (the Indian National Congress formed in 1885), the decades of electoral activity, albeit under a restricted franchise, and the early recruitment of Indians into the judiciary and the elite Indian Civil Service. India at independence possessed an experienced cadre of politicians, bureaucrats, and others who were attuned and committed to liberal democratic principles and rules (Brown 1985: 342–3).

In Africa, the indigenous population in Senegal has had an

unusually long history of protodemocratic contestation. French imperialism was relatively enlightened in this, its oldest African colony. France created four urban communes in Senegal in 1848, thereby conferring the rights of French citizenship on their inhabitants. Political activity and electoral competition date from 1871. Deputies from Senegal served in the French National Assembly thereafter. In 1898, the first non-European won election from Senegal as a deputy in Paris. A relatively advanced educational system, though based on the French model, sought to assimilate the Senegalese to French culture. French-style education and long-established liberal institutions account in part for the vibrancy of electoral politics and the Senegalese elite's pugnacious defence of civil liberties.

However, the absence of a protodemocratic colonial experience does not preclude post-colonial democracy. Botswana, a small country in Southern Africa, did not have a Legislative Council until 1961 – and even then only a third of the members were Africans and they were selected by chief-dominated African Councils. The first election under adult suffrage was held only in October 1965, less than a year before independence. Elected local councils were established only in 1966. If, however, the colonial experience was uncongenial to democracy, a precolonial tradition of freedom of assembly and expression does provide a foundation. The *kgotla* is a traditional institution of the Tswana peoples, who constitute about three-quarters of the country's population of 1.2 million people. Originally a communal meeting in which adult males could question their chiefs and voice their opinions on local concerns, it continues today as a forum of men and women in which politicians and civil servants can gauge public support for contemplated or ongoing programmes. The continuing vitality of this institution imparts a distinctive indigenous flavour to Botswana's political system.

Insofar as the political traditions of most African countries are both hierarchical and heterogeneous, the inherited norms and values do not facilitate democratic consolidation. Nonetheless, astute leaders may interpret these traditions in a manner that supports their own vision. This is what the African socialists did in the early days. There are usually elements of precolonial institutions that, with some creativity, can be adapted to fit contemporary democratic systems. Of particular relevance are the traditional mechanisms to dissuade or sanction despotic leadership.

If civil society is fragmented and weak, this will also hinder democratic consolidation. Political parties, free competitive elections, and
the enforcement of the rule of law are all essential to democratic
transitions. But the survival of these institutions depends upon the
emergence of a strong civil society, that is, upon the emergence of a
dense network of autonomous civil associations and of a social
consensus on democratic political values. Without committed and
vigilant civil associations, parties will again deteriorate into associations of self-seekers, electoral opponents will have recourse to
violence and the rigging of elections, and bureaucrats and judges will
manipulate the law for partisan or personal advantage.

Fragmented or organizationally underdeveloped sub-Saharan
societies have been vulnerable to authoritarian reversals. Ethnic,
regional, and religious cleavages fragment civil society in some
cases. Class identities and organizations that elsewhere have supported liberal democracy are weak. Yet civil society cannot be
reduced to class and communal categories alone; it comprises, as
well, occupational, grassroots, and issue-oriented associations.
Some of the latter have courageously championed human rights and
representative institutions, sometimes to dramatic effect, as a later
section will show.

Deep communal cleavages will complicate or even undermine the
give-and-take of democratic competition. Electoral politics will
tend to exacerbate divisions if ambitious politicians appeal to communal identities and suspicions in order to garner support. When
political parties mirror regional, ethnic, or religious cleavages, the
principal danger arises. People will then tend to interpret the victory
of a particular party or coalition as the victory of one ethnic/regional
or religious group over the others. This perception corrodes the
mutual trust between the 'ins' and the 'outs' on which democratic
politics depends, and threatens a decline into communal violence.
Such a dynamic largely accounts for the demise of Nigeria's First
Republic in 1966, and the brevity of Sudan's constitutional interlude
under Prime Minister El Sadiq el-Mahdi (1986–9), for example.
Autocrats have made much of this divisiveness in their denunciations of multiparty politics.

However, ethnic/regional/religious heterogeneity does not inevitably breed mutual mistrust and democratic breakdowns. Senegal,
Gambia, Botswana, and Mauritius are all socially heterogeneous,
yet generally non-violent, multiparty electoral competitions

continue. One unifying condition is an 'overarching element of cultural unity' (Diamond 1988c: 12). Although Senegal and Gambia both comprise several major ethnic groups, with none forming a majority of the population, Islam performs an integrative role by providing common symbols, life-styles, and a sense of identity to most citizens. National identity is relatively strong in Senegal (except in the region of Casamance) owing to its long history as a colony and independent country. In Botswana the Setswana language and common cultural traditions constitute a basis of unity for the majority of the population who belong to the Tswana tribes. The government's policy of 'ethnic arithmetic' – distributing cabinet positions and public services on a regionally equitable basis – also helps preserve civility.

Also, if a political party or coalition of parties draws support across communal lines, it may serve as a forum for bargaining and reconciliation among groups. The Indian Congress Party at its best has played this role. Alternatively, as in Malaysia, communally based parties may form a coalition in the knowledge that the alternative to cooperation is communal violence, to the detriment of all. Political leaders are not simply at the mercy of communal forces; enlightened constitutional arrangements and accommodations can reconcile social heterogeneity with electoral competition.

This reconciliation is what Nigerians sought to achieve in designing the institutions of the Second Republic – not unsuccessfully according to some (Diamond 1988b: 65) – and seek today in the transition to the Third Republic. Many Nigerians voice the fear that the current two-party system will aggravate religious/ethnic polarization (Akinola 1989: 109–23). Mob attacks on Christians in northern cities have grown over the past decade. If the two parties mirror the north–south, Muslim–Christian divide, the prospects for peaceful democratic competition are bleak. Cognizant of this danger, Nigeria's constitutional engineers have sought to ensure a balance of power between north and south, Muslim and Christian. The constitution of the Third Republic, like that of the Second, compels the contesting parties and presidential candidates to obtain a minimum level of support outside any regional stronghold.

Multiparty democracy and national unity are not inherently antithetical. As one comparative study lightly concludes: 'in dealing with ethnic disunity, when democracy is good it is very, very good,

and when it is bad, it makes bad ethnic problems even worse'
(Douglas 1972: 52).

The weakness of classes that have elsewhere championed democracy may also obstruct democratic consolidation. One classical
theory identifies a strong and independent bourgeoisie as a necessary condition of liberal democracy. As Milton Friedman succinctly
phrases the case in *Capitalism and Freedom* (1962: 9), '[t]he kind of
economic organization that provides economic freedom directly,
namely, competitive capitalism, also promotes political freedom
because it separates economic power from political power and in
this way enables the one to offset the other'. This is not only a theory
of doctrinaire liberals. The radical sociologist Barrington Moore, in
his celebrated exploration of the historical roots of democracy and
dictatorship, concludes that 'a vigorous and independent class of
town dwellers has been an indispensable element in the growth of
parliamentary democracy. No bourgeois, no democracy' (Moore
1966: 418). And the Marxist Samir Amin contends that the pattern
of capitalist evolution at the periphery blocks 'autocentric accumulation', thereby rendering 'true bourgeois democratization' practically unrealizable (Amin 1987: 5).

So Africa's stunted and dependent capitalism shapes stunted and
dependent class relations. A large and impoverished peasantry, a
small industrial working class, an expanding urban sub-proletariat,
and a tiny privileged group of largely state-dependent businessmen,
bureaucrats, politicians, professionals, and landowners, as one sees
in much of Africa, is not a class structure that disperses power or
facilitates accommodation. No self-confident business class with an
independent economic base – that is, no hegemonic bourgeoisie –
disciplines the holders of political power. Instead, mass poverty and
the substantial dependence of wealth upon the acquisition of political power transform political struggles into a deadly zero-sum
game. Victors gain access to economic resources as well as power;
losers have virtually no alternative avenues of upward mobility. In
this atmosphere electoral competition easily degenerates into a fran-
tic and violent fight.

Some commentators thus applaud the current structural adjustment programmes, believing that the rejuvenation of the private
sector furthers social pluralism by separating economic from political power. '[T]he increasing movement away from statist economic
policies and structures,' claims one expert, 'is among the most

significant boosts to the democratic prospect in Africa' (Diamond 1988c: 27). But this is overly sanguine. Structural adjustment entails an economic austerity that may intensify the struggles for scarce resources. And Third World bourgeoisies are, in any event, not always democratic champions. As the Brazilian sociologist Fernando Cardoso points out, the Brazilian bourgeoisie, though relatively large and independent, nonetheless supported bureaucratic authoritarianism in the 1960s and much of the 1970s. It was only a late and mild opponent of Brazilian dictatorship (Cardoso 1986: 150–1). Business leaders will support repression, if they fear the backlash that vast inequalities, mass poverty, and simmering discontents may breed. Unless carefully managed, political liberalization will call existing property and power relations into question.

If rapid economic growth accompanies economic liberalization, the democratic prospect improves. It is significant that successive waves of democratization and authoritarianism in Latin America corresponded, until the 1980s, to trends in the global economy (Therborn 1979: 87–9). Depression or recession in the advanced capitalist countries translates into severe economic and hence political difficulties in most peripheral countries. Growth in the private sector, on the other hand, lessens the premium on political power, and eases social tensions by raising living standards. In India modest though steady growth and a large middle class centred on the private sector have meant that many opportunities exist for ambitious individuals outside of politics. However, sustained growth remains elusive in contemporary Africa. That two of the sub-continent's best economic performers, Botswana and Mauritius, are among the handful of established liberal democracies is unlikely to be a coincidence.

Global capitalism, in sum, is hardly an unmitigated blessing for Third World liberal democracy.

Global geopolitics and foreign influences have frustrated, but also in some cases promoted, African democratization. On the one hand, Western democracies, especially France and the United States, and the Soviet Union were notorious for their willingness to buttress friendly African dictators during the heyday of the Cold War. On the other hand, pro-Western political (semi-)democracies such as Senegal, Botswana, and Mauritius have long reaped their rewards in the form of generous aid and benevolent consideration within international financial institutions. Moreover, the recent trend to attach political, in addition to economic, conditions to African assistance has augmented the leverage of indigenous democratic activists.

France has maintained an unusually pervasive influence in its former colonies of West and Central Africa and in other franco-phone countries, including Zaire. French governments until 1990 showed no compunction in supporting autocrats who upheld French commercial and strategic interests. France exerted its influence through cultural, economic, and military channels. It has devoted substantial resources to maintain educational systems in the former colonies modelled on the French system, including the secondment of French secondary and university teachers under aid agreements. It has exercised economic influence by concentrating its considerable official development assistance and foreign investment on its former colonies, and by continuing to sponsor a franc zone encompassing former colonies even though this arrangement has proved costly. Finally, France has entered into defence or military assistance agreements with its African allies. These agreements have permitted France to prop up one-party governments in Côte d'Ivoire, Gabon, Niger, and Benin. In August 1983, socialist President François Mitterrand mounted one of the largest French military operations in Africa since the Algerian war of the 1960s. Code-named Operation Manta, this intervention involved the commitment of 3,000 troops and substantial weaponry to Chad to protect a friendly warlord against Libyan and Libyan-backed insurgents. The bulk of the troops withdrew in 1984. Significantly, they were not recommitted to defeat another Libyan-backed incursion in late 1990, and consequently, the Hissèn Habré government was overthrown by the forces of Idris Deby.

Only in the late 1980s did Mitterrand move away from the traditional French policy of support for pro-French one-party and military governments (Whiteman 1988: 50–4). Popular discontent was one factor influencing the shift in policy. In 1990, Benin, Gabon, Côte d'Ivoire, Cameroon, Burundi, and Chad suffered severe internal unrest or invasions by insurgents. Other factors that stiffened French resolve were the manifest inability of their corrupt African partners to grapple successfully with prolonged economic crisis, the end of the Cold War, and the growing integration of French interests with those of the European Community. France responded by distancing itself from its autocratic allies. Mitterand refused a request from Houphouet-Boigny in mid-1990 to put down a mutiny of Ivoirien army conscripts who were protesting their conditions. Since the Ivoirien president was the *doyen* of francophone Africa, the message was clear. It was driven home by Foreign Minister Roland Dumas in rejecting French intervention against the Chadian insurgents: 'The time has passed when France could pick and choose the governments in these countries, change them, or maintain them as it wished' (Whiteman 1991: 5). African autocrats, left on their own, have had to come to terms with their rebellious citizens. Hence, a wave of political liberalization has swept francophone countries, mostly in the form of promised multiparty elections.

Zaire is a case in which democratic movements had long to contend with French, US, and Belgian support for the autocratic Mobutu Sese-Seko before 1990 (Willame 1988: 43–4). Zaire's size, strategic location in Central Africa, reserves of important metals, and surreptitious aid to UNITA, the US-supported insurgents in formerly Marxist–Leninist Angola, largely accounted for the Western solicitude. Probably no Western government felt comfortable buttressing a leader whose government was renowned for its corruption, maladministration, and oppressiveness. But fear of who might take over from the pro-Western Mobutu motivated the reluctant external support. Consequently, the regime's Western allies arranged nine reschedulings of Zaire's external debt since 1978, even though a substantial portion of the infusions of hard currencies were redirected to the private overseas accounts of prominent political insiders. The Israelis, Americans, and West Germans trained Mobutu's presidential guard, and they and other allies transferred repression technology to Zaire's army and security police. When rebels invaded Shaba province in 1977 and again in 1978, the Belgians, Americans, and Moroccans cooperated to repulse the attacks. All these moves relieved the pressure on Mobutu to come to terms with dissident elements.

Only when, in 1990, his Western patrons signalled their unwillingness to continue in that role did Mobutu begin to come to terms with the Zairean opposition. But Mobutu's efforts to manipulate the democratic transition to his own advantage led to the virtual collapse of his authority in late 1991.

Equatorial Guinea constitutes an extreme example of the baneful political influence of foreign powers (Liniger-Goumaz 1988). Franco's Spain served as a role model for this small former Spanish colony in West Africa. The constitution inherited at independence in 1968 was essentially an 'enabling act' for authoritarian rule; it provided for a highly centralized power structure. To make matters worse, the Spanish authorities chose as their successor an unstable and semi-literate but ostensibly malleable civil servant, Francesco Macias Nguema. The Spanish miscalculated: within a year, the insecurity in the country compelled the Spanish government to evacuate its citizens. A reign of terror then commenced, which persisted for a decade. Even then, foreign powers jockeyed for influence in this small country, owing to its mineral and agricultural wealth. Macias turned to the Soviet Union as its principal external patron, after relations with Spain soured. Finally, with the economy in ruins and much of the population in exile, the dictator was overthrown and executed in 1979. Obiang Nguema, the military leader, shifted his country back to a pro-Western orientation and undertook structural adjustment. Yet it was not until the fading of the Cold War in the late 1980s that outside sponsors pressured the regime to end human-rights abuses.

Not only Western countries engaged in such counterrevolutionary activities. South Africa's covert campaign in the 1980s to destabilize Angola, Mozambique, and Zimbabwe was a further blow to peaceful political reform and accommodation in these countries. The same could be said of the Soviet Union's support for the murderous Macias. As well, the Soviet Union's heavy military and economic aid to the oppressive Mengistu regime in Ethiopia reduced the latter's need to compromise with its enemies. Only since the change of mood that accompanied the winding down of the Cold War have autocratic regimes had to contemplate reforms. Even the Soviet Union advised its former clients – Ethiopia, Angola, and Mozambique – to join the IMF, accommodate internal enemies, and undertake economic and political liberalization.

'Political conditionality' may also impel or hasten democratic transitions. It is increasingly common for international and national aid agencies to attach requirements for political reforms to loan and grant agreements. In the case of Kenya, for instance, the US Congress in November 1990 specified four conditions that the country would have to meet to receive military aid: charge or release political prisoners; improve treatment of prisoners; restore freedom of the judiciary; and restore freedom of expression. Then, in November 1991, Kenya's aid donors collectively suspended new aid pledges for six months to pressure President Daniel arap Moi into democratic reform. The US Congress also suspended all economic and military assistance to former allies such as Liberia, Somalia, Sudan, and Zaire which had poor human-rights records.[3]

Political conditionality raises mixed feelings in Africa. Although the external focus on human-rights issues assists beleaguered democratic activists, it irritates them with its paternalistic and ethnocentric tone. Foreigners patronize Africans by purporting to protect them from the folly, oppressiveness, and corruption of their leaders. One unfortunate dimension of the current consensus is that it encourages Western officials to blame Africa's problems almost wholly on Africans, namely, on wrong policies and corrupt, inefficient governance. This simplistic proposition, once accepted, permits Western governments to posture as the champions of the wretched of the earth – and without increasing their niggardly flows of aid. Many African regimes desperately need generous economic assistance to carry through unpopular programmes of economic liberalization. But, instead of increasing aid, the donors demand that additional political reforms be undertaken in order for countries to receive the same volume of assistance. To democratize in the midst of severe economic deprivation is a daunting task, even for the well-intentioned. Finally, the new democratic missionaries are perceived as ethnocentric in assuming the innate superiority of Western-style, liberal-democratic institutions.

If in the short run political conditionality will lever desperate regimes into political liberalization, in the long run its political efficacy is problematical. Kwesi Botchwey, Ghana's finance secretary, made this point elegantly in a 1990 speech to the African Development Bank. 'What is at issue,' he declared:

is not whether African countries should democratise or not, for democratisation is clearly in the objective interests of African Development. What is at issue is whether it should evolve, or be preserved through essentially internal or endogenous processes with the African people themselves finding their own forms of organization and means of struggle against oppression, or whether it should come about as a condition of external financial assistance and in the form of a checklist of standard institutional arrangements rooted in the alien experience of other countries. (*West Africa* 25 June–1 July 1990: 1065)

In the latter case, the new 'democratic' leaders would be mere puppets dancing to a foreign tune. A neo-colonial relationship would undercut popular support for the imported democratic institutions.

Although historical, cultural, socio-economic, and international conditions are generally (though not uniformly or wholly) unfavourable to democratic consolidation, one should not jump to the conclusion that authoritarianism is inevitable. A country can lack most of the facilitative conditions, yet still achieve stable democracy. Botswana is a case in point:

[T]raditional political structures at the tribal level were highly authoritarian. Colonial rule did almost nothing to encourage or provoke new forms of citizen political organization. The social class structure is highly skewed, with a large low-income category, a small middle class, and a minuscule group of wealthy cattle owners... Approximately 80 percent of the population is not literate. Transportation and communications are poor... The economy is dominated by state planning and foreign investment. Since independence, only a very small number of politically active interest groups have developed outside of, possibly, the trade union area. (Holm 1988: 202)

Yet Botswana has benefited from a rights-protective, multiparty, system for twenty-five years.

Domestic political factors, especially a skilled and committed leadership and a politically mobilized civil society, can mitigate conditions hostile to democracy. The historical, cultural, socio-economic, and global conditions constrain but do not determine political outcomes. Leaders, social movements, and civil associations still have some room for manoeuvre.

Skilful leadership, in the pliable circumstances of the first generation of independence, has a greater impact in shaping political life than in more institutionalized polities. Despite unfavourable circumstances, shrewd leaders have sometimes succeeded in implanting democratic institutions, imperfect though they are. Although such leaders are more often motivated by self-preservation than altruism, the outcome may nonetheless be beneficial to the citizenry.

Skilful leadership has been an important ingredient in Botswana's democratic development. Sir Seretse Khama, the first prime minister and president, and his lieutenants in the Botswana Democratic Party

(BDP) sought the legitimacy and international prestige that democratic institutions confer. Legitimacy was a potential problem because the bureaucratic state bequeathed by colonialism, though efficient, was overwhelmingly staffed by expatriates. There were few qualified Tswana to whom the government could cede decision-making power without compromising the state's ability to function. Opting for efficiency therefore meant that the government would continue to rely upon expatriates. However, to avoid the appearance of neo-colonialism, the BDP's leaders pragmatically maintained democratic institutions in order to give the people a sense of control.

Electoral competition was, in any event, unlikely to threaten the BDP's hold on power. Owing to the extreme underdevelopment of Botswana and the survival of traditional institutions, the government was not confronted with an array of mobilized and demanding groups. Moreover, the governing elite calculated that an unusually high rate of economic growth would allow it to remain popular by conferring some material benefits on all sections of the population. Thus, the advantages of political democracy outweighed the probable costs (Holm 1988: 202–4; Parson 1984: 51–3).

Consider also the Senegalese case. Redemocratization in Senegal in the mid-1970s is inexplicable without reference to the calculations and actions of Léopold Senghor. The president, undictatorial and tolerant even during the period of one-party rule, might have responded to the waning popularity of his Union Progressiste Sénégalais (UPS) in the time-honoured way – by increasing coercion. Poor economic performance, rising prices, the ending of France's preferential price for Senegalese groundnuts, and drought had alienated first the students and workers in the cities (1968–9), and then the peanut-growing peasantry (in the early 1970s). By the mid-1970s, the government lacked the resources to coopt the rising opposition through the distribution of patronage. Instead of resorting to force, Senghor reacted to public disaffection by unilaterally imposing a new multiparty constitution. He apparently calculated that his renamed Parti Socialiste (PS) could, via political liberalization, renew its legitimacy and win international prestige and assistance without losing power. The divisions and disorganization of the opposition groups, together with the continued support for the PS by the rural notables and patrons (the so-called *marabouts d'arachides*), minimized the threat of multiparty competition (Coulon 1988: 153–7;

Fatton 1987: 12–13, 160–1). By passing power in 1980 to Abdou Diouf, a lieutenant who shared his liberal approach, Senghor ensured that the democratic experiment would outlive his presidency.

Nigeria provides a dramatic contemporary example of a country in which a political leader is carefully managing a transition to 'democracy'. Major-General Ibrahim Babangida has established the time-table (1989–92) and phases of the transition. His regime appointed a Constitutional Review Commission in 1987 to recommend a constitution for the Third Republic in line with a government white paper. In 1988 Babangida formed a partly appointed, partly elected Constituent Assembly to deliberate upon the Commission's draft constitution. Certain key features, including federalism, presidentialism, and the two-party system, were not however open to discussion. Even then, some of the Assembly's recommendations were rejected or modified in the constitution promulgated by the government in 1989. Babangida has also barred all former politicians from political life, in the belief that earlier democratic experiments failed owing to the moral and personality defects of the leaders. Finally, he not only banned all parties except a Social Democratic Party and a National Republican Convention, but also supplied each party with its manifesto. One he located 'a little to the left', and the other 'a little to the right' in the political spectrum. Time will tell whether such a stage-managed transition can garner the requisite public support.

Popular movements and associations represent another significant factor in the establishment of democracy. In Western countries, the extension of the franchise and other political reforms in the nineteenth and twentieth centuries were largely piecemeal concessions to popular protest. The recent redemocratization in South America also owed much to a 'democratic resistance' to military rule by, among others, the Catholic Church, the underground press, lawyers' and writers' associations, organized labour, and such *ad hoc* groups as 'mothers of the *desapareicidos* (disappeared)' and amnesty committees (Cardoso 1987: 31). Democracy, by becoming a concern of ordinary people, became an irresistible force.

African radicals emphasize the importance of popular mobilization for democracy to take root, but they also acknowledge its limitations in the African context. Noted Nigerian political scientist and activist Claude Ake observes that '[r]ights, especially those that have any real significance for our lives are usually taken, not given – with the cooperation of those in power if possible, but without it if necessary. That is the way it was for other peoples and that is the way it is going to be in Africa' (Ake 1987: 11). Yet, in another publication, Ake laments that African tyrannies have crushed independent, national associations. Ordinary people 'see the state as a hostile force to be evaded, cheated or defeated as circumstances permit. Consequently, loyalties are focused on local communities and primary groups which are often very caring and never threatening. In effect, what is happening in Africa is the dissolution of society rather than its development' (Ake 1990: 591). A vicious circle comes into play. As another African political scientist observes, 'workers, artisans, small traders and small farmers are not politically organized because there is no democracy; but there can be no democracy because the people are not organized' (Nolutshungu 1990: 111–12).

Of particular significance is the paucity and weakness of 'intermediary' institutions that link civil society to the state. Political parties, interest groups, and the mass media elsewhere transmit demands and information between the civil and political spheres. But in Africa they have typically served to secure a compliant rather than a vigilant civil society.

Consider the role of the mass media. Ideally, a free press, radio, and television enhances democracy by monitoring the performance of governments and publicizing abuse of power. In most sub-Saharan countries, however, radio and television broadcasting has been almost exclusively a governmental monopoly. And the press has been limited in readership and subject to state control (Wilcox 1982: 209–32). In 1980, only about ninety daily newspapers were published in sub-Saharan countries, representing merely 1 per cent of the world's daily newspaper circulation. The region also boasted only about 3 per cent of the globe's radio receivers and 1 per cent of its television sets. All the mass media were highly controlled, with the exception of few countries such as Senegal and Nigeria. About 90 per cent of Africa's daily newspapers were owned by an agency of the state or the governing party. Even the few privately owned newspapers had to contend with other forms of regime control: public ownership of printing presses, governmental allocation of newsprint, public subsidies to state-owned newspapers, banning of offensive publications, and harassment or detention of critical journalists. Not surprisingly, therefore, the most forthright, informative, and non-doctrinaire African press was to be found, not in Africa, but in London and Paris. *Jeune Afrique* and *Afrique-Asie* in Paris, and *West Africa*, *Africa* and *The New African* in London, headed the list.

The experience of *The Pioneer*, Ghana's oldest surviving private newspaper, is illustrative of the trials which African journalists have had to endure. It was established in 1939 in Kumasi. Ironically, its glorious days of independence and outspokenness did not long survive the end of colonial rule in 1957. As *West Africa* noted on the occasion of the newspaper's fiftieth anniversary in 1989, '[i]t had been censored, its editors brutalized or jailed without trial, banned, intimidated or, some of the time when tolerated, starved of inputs' (*West Africa* 2–8 Oct. 1989: 63). The newspaper's former editor alluded to these problems in an interview from exile in 1986. He acknowledged that he and the other writers had not lived up to their newspaper's promise to publish 'The Whole Truth.' Why did they practice self-censorship?

First the will to live longer superseded all considerations. I censored myself; I censored everybody working under me; and everyone working under me censored himself. Secondly, we censored ourselves for purely economic reasons. We knew that our ability to eat depended on our ability to publish. Our ability to publish depended on our ability to buy newsprint. And our ability to buy newsprint depended on the benevolence of the good people at the Ministry of Information and the Castle [Chairman Flt.-Lieut. Jerry Rawlings' office]. (Ankomah 1986: 34)

Since Ghana has not ranked among the most oppressive environments in Tropical Africa, these words are eloquent testimony to the travails of journalists throughout the region.

Fortunately, the recent liberalizing trend has entailed greater official tolerance of free expression. In East Africa, for example, Uganda, Tanzania, and Kenya were all for many years bereft of independent reportage. But that changed in the 1980s.

In Uganda, the overthrow of the tyrannical Idi Amin in 1979 created a limited opening for independent reportage. Two newspapers – *Weekly Topic* and *Munansi* – and two magazines – *Forward* and *Mawazo* – took on the challenge of exposing President Milton

Obote's growing authoritarianism between 1980 and 1985. Following the victory of the National Resistance Army in early 1986, the independent press turned to monitor any oligarchical tendencies in the NRM regime. Its earlier opposition to the opponents of the National Resistance Movement has legitimated its rights to assume a critical stance.

In Tanzania, the government has permitted three private newspapers to publish since 1988. *Business Times, Family Mirror,* and *Fahari* (Bull) are widely perceived as the 'opposition' press – and indeed they have provided a forum for public criticism of the government and ruling party. President Moi's government in Kenya has been less flexible. Although several private newspapers have circulated in this country for many decades, they have shown few sparks of independence since the late 1970s. The task of debating political and constitutional reforms fell, until the political liberalization of December 1991, to certain Christian publications and three private magazines – *Society, Finance,* and the *Nairobi Law Monthly.* Intimidation of the editors and banning of the periodicals were common events by the late 1980s.

Although often deprived of independent information, some civil associations have struggled to maintain their autonomy even in the context of single-party and military regimes. Africans have not been without means of resistance to authoritarian tendencies.

Consider the variety of people's organizations and voluntary organizations that have emerged. Some associations are in a sense parochial, such as village improvement societies, umbrella bodies of community-based groups, kinship organizations, or ethnic unions, though their frequent emphasis on self-help builds a sense of efficacy as well as material improvement. Others are national organizations to advance particular interests – trade unions, students' associations, professional societies, trades' groups, cooperatives, and so on. Gender is a third basis of organization. Though governments have sought to control women's associations, often by implanting the president's wife as chair of the official association, unofficial and more militant women's groups have also emerged in many countries. A final category is associations based upon conviction: 'green' associations, human-rights organizations, religious movements, both Muslim and Christian.

Associational life in Africa received a fillip in the postwar period (Chazan 1982). The emergent trade unions, cooperatives, ethnic unions, women's organizations, and professional and student associations were in many instances the precursors of the nationalist parties. After independence, authoritarian regimes sought to control these civil associations. However, some of them retained a modicum of independence. These, along with village and neighbourhood development associations, sports clubs, church groups, and rotating credit associations, remained popular because they continued to supply an important service. Some of them have also played, and continue to play, an important role in channelling popular discontent.

Consider a few instances. In Senegal, though President Senghor guided the democratic transition in 1974–6, he was prodded into action by the publicly demonstrated disaffection of workers, students, and farmers, and by the acute criticism of the politically engaged intelligentsia. In Sudan, a coalition of professional, academic, and trade union associations – the National Alliance for National Salvation – was instrumental in ousting dictator Jaafar Nimeiri in April 1985 and negotiating a one-year transition to general elections and civilian rule. Unfortunately, the democratic interlude was brief and chaotic. An Association of Recognized Professional Bodies with a similar composition united to oppose General I.K. Acheampong in Ghana in the mid-1970s. A nation-wide strike in July 1977, involving professionals as well as workers and students, prompted a palace coup. Although Acheampong's successor negotiated a transition to multiparty elections, civilian rule endured for only two years.

In Nigeria, an array of civil associations, intellectuals, and opinion leaders has championed human rights and accountable government in the 1980s (Diamond 1988b: 71). Particularly vigilant and vocal were the following organizations: the Nigerian Academic Staff Union, the National Association of Nigerian Students, the Nigerian Bar Association, the Nigerian Medical Association, the Nigerian Labour Congress, Women in Nigeria, the National Organization of Nigerian Women Societies, the Nigerian Union of Journalists, and the Nigerian Chamber of Commerce. Periodically, some of these associations have coalesced in social movements to demand political reform. In 1982, for instance, the National Association of Nigerian Students, Women in Nigeria, some socialist parties and radical intellectuals formed the Alliance for Democratic Rights. This protested against the corruption, ethnic chauvinism, and disregard for democratic norms of Shehu Shagari's civilian government. Following the 1983 coup, the Alliance demanded that Major-General Muhammadu Buhari rescind a series of oppressive decrees. Buhari, in turn, was deposed in 1985. Buhari's successor, Major-General Ibrahim Babangida, announced that human rights was a priority for his regime. Two civil rights associations, the Committee for the Defence of Human Rights and the Civil Liberties Organization, have periodically infuriated the regime by alleging rights violations or legally challenging the government. A Committee for Unity and Progress, formed in 1989 to canvas alternatives to the government's structural adjustment programme, has been equally annoying. Although Babangida blocked its conference on structural adjustment, the organization (composed of professional associations, the university students, and Women in Nigeria among others) has since campaigned for a speedier democratic transition.

Nigerian civil society is clearly far from defenceless. However, many officials of these civil associations have had to suffer intimidation by the security forces, detention, and mistreatment for their activities.

The same is true in Kenya. Since his accession to the presidency in 1978, Daniel arap Moi has progressively weakened the independence of the press, the judiciary, the auditor-general, the civil service, the electoral system, the national assembly, and the mass organizations, especially the Central Organization of Trade Unions (Kenya) and Mandaleo Wa Wanawake, the national women's organization. Yet some individuals have protested the authoritarian trend. University students, some intellectuals, church leaders, and lawyers have been the regime's most consistent critics. Yet these critics received little space in the intimidated private press – until the government's reluctant acceptance of a multiparty system in December 1991. Sycophancy had reigned hitherto, to the secret disgust of many Kenyans.

When two wealthy former cabinet ministers, Charles Rubia and Kenneth Matiba, publicly advocated the legalization of opposition parties in July 1990, dissent had entered a new phase. The banning of their rally and the detention of the two dissenters precipitated four days of rioting and looting in Nairobi and five provincial capitals. This revolt reflected the widespread hostility to the heavy-handed, corrupt, and ethnically biased rule of the Kenya African National Union (KANU), and the extensive unemployment (Shields 1990:

16). Moi, though firmly rejecting a multiparty constitutional system, initiated a reform commission within KANU. In December 1990, he endorsed several minor reforms that did not satisfy the growing democratic opposition. Only under intense pressure a year later did Moi finally legalize opposition parties.

In Côte d'Ivoire, more extensive unrest associated with a sharper economic crisis compelled earlier concessions to the democratic movement than in Kenya. Three months of sporadic strikes and street demonstrations erupted in Abidjan in February 1990. Economic grievances initially sparked this unprecedented strife. Abidjan University students demonstrated to publicize a range of university-related grievances. The union of university faculty supported the students, but went further in demanding an overhaul of the country's educational system, a reversal of the government's austerity policies, and a repatriation of the leaders' ill-gotten funds illegally stashed abroad. Civil servants protested a wage freeze and new taxes. By March, the demonstrators, who now included thousands of schoolchildren and others, brandished signs denouncing President Houphouet-Boigny and demanding multiparty elections. Repression plus concessions on salary issues and the proposed tax hike did not stem the unrest. Only the announcement in April of the legalization of twenty-five opposition parties and the scheduling of free elections in October and November 1990 brought peace. In the event, a chastened Houphouet-Boigny and Parti Democratique de Côte d'Ivoire (PDCI) managed to win the elections – with the help of some intimidation of opponents, vilification of the opposition in the government media, and electoral malpractices (Bourke 1991: 15–16). The PDCI rediscovered Senghor's stratagem: that even an unpopular governing party has the resources at its disposal to defeat a divided opposition.

Denunciations of governmental abuse, demonstrations, strikes, and riots constitute the visible face of the assertion of civil society; but one should not overlook the everyday forms of resistance to oppression. These include participation in the black market and smuggling networks, withdrawal from cash-crop production, emigration, 'rumour-mongering' about official malfeasance, and satirical or critical popular theatre, songs, and literary expression.

Popular culture as a form of protest is a largely unexplored phenomenon. Plays performed by ordinary people in indigenous languages have proved a powerful medium for consciousness-raising about injustice and repression. In Kenya, for example, the novelist and playwright Ngugi wa Thiong'o participated with others in writing and producing two such critical plays in the 1980s. Both were scripted in local languages, employed untrained actors, and were soon banned by the authorities. *I Will Marry When I Want* involved the collaboration of hundreds of residents of Kamiriithu (just to the north of Nairobi), many of whom were illiterate industrial workers, agricultural labourers, and the unemployed. The play became part of a literacy programme. The local people not only built the theatre, but acted in and helped refine the play. It became highly popular, drawing people from Nairobi even for rehearsals. In response, the government banned the play, and closed down the theatre. Ngugi's second venture, *Mother, Sing for Me*, transcended the Kikuyu medium of the first play by using five Kenyan languages. It was to be staged in Nairobi's National Theatre. But Moi's insecure government banned the play before it even opened. Those who attended the rehearsals professed to being touched by the play – what they had known as individuals they re-experienced collectively (Bjorkman 1989). Ngugi soon went into exile in London.

Pop songs are an even more potent medium of protest, for they reach a much larger audience than popular theatre. Pop singers have crystallized popular resentment, though to escape banning and arrest they often cultivate ambiguity. The Nigerian, Fela Anikulapo-Kuti, however, has abjured this protection. He has twice been jailed, once for almost a year, for his condemnations of official corruption, political repression, and subservience to neo-colonialism. In April 1989 the government deployed 1,000 heavily armed police to abort one of his concerts in Abeokuta. University students, in particular, rally to songs (written in pidgin) such as 'Beasts of No Nation':

> Animal talk done start again:
> 'Dash them human rights.'
> How animal go know say they no born me as slave?
> How animal go know say slave trade done pass?
> And they want dash us human rights...
> Human rights na my property
> You can't dash me my property.[4]

Poets and novelists, too, have produced satires or exposes of post-colonial (and colonial) political abuses. Since they normally write in a European language, the middle classes and university students form the main audience. But the limited domestic audience has not stopped insecure autocrats from banning offensive works and detaining even their authors. Ngugi wa Thiong'o spent a stint in detention, and Jack Mpanje, Malawi's foremost poet, has languished in prison for many years for allusive poetry deemed scurrilous by President-for-Life Dr Hastings Banda. Luckily for Okot p'Bitek, he published 'Song of Prisoner' in 1971, before Kenya entered its less tolerant period under President Moi. It is unlikely that the latter would have tolerated these critical thoughts:

> What is Uhuru
> When all my thoughts
> Are deep and silent rivers
> Blocked up by concrete walls
> Of fear and black suspicions?
>
> How can I think freely
> When the very air
> Has ears larger than
> Those of the elephant
> And keener than the bones
> Of the *ngege* fish?
> (Okot p'Bitek 1971: 90)

'Rumour-mongering', or *radio trottoir* as it is called in francophone Africa, is another everyday form of resistance to authoritarianism. Where governments directly or indirectly control the mass media, rumours allow people to circumvent official channels of communication. Why apparently strong dictatorships devote so much energy to denouncing and threatening those who purportedly 'mislead' the public is a mystery to outsiders. Official fears, however, are not misguided: the 'wild' rumours often have a basis in fact. People in the street soon learn about the machinations, indiscretions, and illicit dealings of their rulers. Worse, informal communications often ridicule the pretensions of the 'big men' and enhance the solidarity of the oppressed. The rumour mill therefore undermines the legitimacy of the regime. It prepares the day of reckoning when the people, apparently spontaneously, take to the streets.

It would be misleading, however, to leave the impression that Africans everywhere wait impatiently to embrace democracy. Actually, disgust at the irresponsibility and venality of politicians and political parties has grown during periodic multiparty experiments. When, in purportedly 'democratic' policies, parties become a refuge for self-seekers, bureaucrats and police are known to be corrupt, judges are often bribed, and soldiers are undisciplined, people come to regard democracy with indifference or even contempt.

The people of Yardaji, a small village on Nigeria's northern border, graphically conveyed their disgust with politicians when they posted this public notice at the outset of the 1983 federal election campaign:

WARNING: WE DON'T WANT IT
The people of Yardaji Have No Regard For Any Political Party Whatsoever. We Are Tired of Hearing Idle Talk. Whoever Ignores This Advice Will Regret It. Listen Well: Don't come Here. This is Not a Matter of One Person Alone. We Don't Want It. (Miles 1987: 65)

Such cynicism enables the incumbent regime to eliminate constitutional safeguards with impunity, or the army to instigate a coup (as happened in Nigeria following the election).

Although cultural and objective conditions are mainly unfavourable to democratization, political factors – in particular, astute leadership, popular mobilization, and external pressure – may compensate for the unfavourable conditions. Democratic transitions will widely occur, but the consolidation of democracy is a longer term and more dubious proposition. This consolidation will depend upon the formation of a vigilant and organized civil society, a process that is dramatically underway in some sub-Saharan countries.

But even if liberal democracy succeeds against the odds in establishing itself, it may not prove as efficacious in socio-economic terms as the new development ideology assumes. Just as the World Bank's *Sub-Saharan Africa* report (1989a) is unrealistic about democratic prospects in Africa, it is overly sanguine about whether more liberal democracies will result in more equitable growth. The relationship is actually more complex: liberal-democratic regimes in the Third World are compatible with respectable growth rates, yet they are less facilitative of equity than is often thought.

Recall that the new consensus which benignly links economic to political liberalization is of recent vintage. For many years conventional wisdom held that, in the early stages of economic development, authoritarian governments were more conducive to growth than democratic ones. A widely used economics textbook written in 1966 alerted readers to 'a cruel choice between rapid (self-sustained) expansion and democratic processes' (Bhagwati 1966: 204). Twenty years later, another writer darkly observes that 'those countries [in the Third World] which cherished and preserved a democratic framework fared much worse than those that adopted a nondemocratic or dictatorial framework. Democracies throughout the Third World have collapsed under the burden of economic stagnation and have given way to dictatorships of either the right or the left' (Rao 1984-5: 67). Dictatorships were thought to be in a better position than democracies to promote growth by: creating the stability and order that investors demand; imposing sacrifices on organized labour in order to keep wage rates competitive; promoting capital accumulation by shifting income to the wealthy business class; and minimizing waste by eliminating or reducing the 'pork-barrel' practices associated with democratic politics.

Although the case for developmental dictatorships appeared plausible, in practice dictatorships have not been high economic achievers. True, some credit the 'Japanese model' of 'soft authoritarianism' with the remarkable economic success of not only Japan, but postwar South Korea, Taiwan, and Singapore as well. A combination of 'absolutist states and capitalist economies', in which the state actively mobilizes the people and corporations behind a coherent, market-based development strategy, is the model's essence (Johnson 1987: 143). But the model's success depends upon stringent conditions: the political ascendancy of a nationalist elite with the will, the autonomy from social forces, and the state capacities to carry through an ambitious, state-orchestrated development programme. Such conditions emerge only in rare historical and cultural circumstances. In Latin America and Africa, where the circumstances are quite different than in East Asia, dictators have generally not succeeded in promoting rapid and sustained economic development (Weinstein 1983; Kohli 1986: 154–60; Hartlyn and Morley 1986).

African experience shows that democracy is congruent with

economic growth in poor countries, contrary to the earlier conventional wisdom. Excluding countries whose growth rates have been skewed because they are major oil exporters or because of their prolonged civil wars, one discovers the following relationship. The four countries with the worst economic performances – those in which per-capita GNP declined at a rate of more than 2 per cent between 1965 and 1985 – were Zaire, Niger, Ghana, and Uganda. All of these had autocratic (and, with the exception of Niger, corrupt and capricious) regimes during most or all of this period. The four countries with the best economic performance – those in which per capita GNP grew at an annual rate of more than 2 per cent – were Lesotho, Cameroon, Botswana, and Mauritius. The last two feature among Africa's handful of multiparty democracies, whereas the first two have had relatively benign authoritarian governments. Democracy and growth are thus compatible, and probably mutually reinforcing.

Yet it is also clear that liberal democracy is no panacea for mismanagement and politically generated inefficiencies. Growth requires a political system that shelters economic managers from the distributive demands and the rent-seeking behaviour of powerful classes and individuals. Such insulation is difficult to achieve in democracies whose officials must periodically court the favour of the public.

India, the Third World's largest and longest-surviving representative democracy, illustrates this vulnerability. A country with a per capita income and degree of social heterogeneity similar to many African countries, India achieved an average annual growth of GNP per capita of 1.8 per cent between 1965 and 1986. Although this record would place the country among the top performers in Africa, many Indian commentators regard this growth rate as sluggish. Economists have explained this 'low' rate of accumulation in terms of policy and political failings. Pranab Bardhan, for example, sees successive governments as captives of an influential coalition of proprietary classes – industrialists, rich farmers, and professionals in the bureaucracy (Bardhan 1984). The low rate and inefficiency of public investment arise largely from governmental efforts to appease these fractious elements. When they squabble (as they constantly do), regimes try to placate them all. Governments thus fritter away resources on high salaries for bureaucrats, high subsidies for farmers, and cheap credit for rural and urban entrepreneurs. And economic problems are compounded by the declining efficiency of a patronage-ridden civil service and growing outlays on the coercive apparatus to maintain order as public disillusion deepens.

Multiparty politics in Africa is similarly unlikely to eliminate the clientelistic basis of unproductive resource allocations and poor public management. However, combined economic and political liberalization may at least restrict the scope of clientelistic criteria while maintaining political stability. Senegal's experience illustrates this possibility (Somerville 1988). Since independence in 1960, the ruling Union Progressiste Sénégalais/Parti Socialiste has retained its support by distributing patronage to key groups – beneficial producer prices for groundnuts, subsidized food, subsidized public services, employment in the civil service and state corporations. Yet drought and other problems in the 1970s reduced the patronage resources of the regime, as did the market-oriented reforms demanded by the IMF and World Bank in exchange for their loans. President Senghor responded by loosening authoritarian controls in 1974–6. The refurbished liberal-democratic constitution, by renewing the regime's legitimacy, allowed the government to survive despite its diminished capacity to purchase electoral support. Clientelism is still very much alive, but it is no longer as pervasive as formerly.

Troubling also is the failure of Third World democracies to introduce much equity, rendering utopian the widely proclaimed goal of 'equitable growth'. There are obvious reasons for expecting elected governments to focus upon the alleviation of mass poverty. The poor's only political resource – their large numbers – should count heavily in a political system characterized by periodic elections and universal adult franchise. This numerical strength should translate, through the ballot box, into beneficial social and economic reforms.

Nevertheless, striking income and wealth disparities persist in representative democracies – and not only in those of the Third World. Poverty and homelessness have become more evident in the larger Western democracies since 1980. Inequality worsened in the United States under Ronald Reagan's presidency, according to the Federal Census Bureau. Between 1977 and 1987, 1 per cent of Americans became 50 per cent richer whereas 80 per cent of the people saw their real incomes decline. While 0.5 per cent of the US population owned almost 40 per cent of the country's wealth in 1987, more than 30 million Americans lived in poverty.

In Latin America and South Asia, democracies have had disappointing welfare records. A comparative study of Costa Rica, Venezuela, and Colombia, three of Latin America's more successful democracies, concludes: 'Liberal democracy in these three cases has been established and maintained in spite of the persistence of profound economic and social inequalities, and there seems to be nothing inherent in liberal democracy that requires serious efforts to reduce or eliminate such inequalities' (Peeler 1985: 129).

The social record of Africa's democracies is similarly undistinguished. In Senegal, relatively open and regular electoral competition fails to safeguard the poor's welfare. Following Senegal's first decade of renewed multiparty semi-democracy, one authority warned of popular disillusion with pluralism and liberalism. This resulted not only from a steadily worsening economic situation, but also from growing inequalities and a poor welfare record even in comparison to other low-income developing countries. Liberal political values appeared 'more and more artificial or theoretical to segments of the population whose daily problems have not been solved by the intellectual debates, games of patronage, and pursuit of international prestige of the Senegalese political class' (Coulon 1988: 161).

In Botswana, rural dwellers – the majority – have benefited from the country's prosperity and democratic politics mainly through effective drought-relief programmes and an increase in such social services as education, health, and clean water. Even here, rural incomes have increased little despite the economic boom. As many as 70 per cent of the population lived below a poverty line as recently as 1987, and those in the rural areas, especially the remnants of the San hunter-gatherers of the Kalahari Desert, were the worst off (Holm 1988: 197–9; and Nowak and Swinehart 1989: 146–7). One commentator concludes that Botswana demonstrates that 'the political equality which elections grant does not lead to any major or even marginal reallocation of economic resources in favor of the poor... [T]he rural population lacks the will, resources, organization, and cultural traditions to take advantage of the opportunities for political power entailed in a national election' (Holm 1982: 100).

Since the poor are the majority in most developing nations, popular sovereignty should mean that they have clout to push for poverty-amelioration programmes and a more equitable pattern of growth. But electoral democracies often fail to do this. This contradiction mirrors the tension inherent in the concept of liberal democracy. Democracy is associated with the ideal of equality, in particular, formal political equality; liberalism champions liberty, especially the right of individuals to accumulate property. In practice, the power of the dominant classes or elites often obstructs state-directed reformism under the guise of defending liberty and the efficacy of market forces. And market relationships, in the absence of a welfare-oriented state, inevitably favour those individuals, firms, and regions that are already richer and better endowed than others, thereby exacerbating inequality.

Although the programme of free enterprise and a market-facilitating, liberal-democratic, minimal state is problematic, it has won wide acceptance among aid donors and acquiescence in Africa. The collapse of collectivist and statist alternatives; the allure of the model's emphasis on equity, sustainability, human rights, decentralization, and popular empowerment; and the powerful global position of its promoters are factors that have contributed to its preponderance.

Certainly, the programme's belated recognition of the merits of democracy and the importance of 'getting the politics right' for economic development is a welcome change. It has contributed to a new political climate in sub-Saharan Africa. But, as argued in this and the previous chapter, the new consensus embodies several unresolved contradictions and unduly sanguine expectations. These weaknesses encourage intellectuals and activists to continue groping for alternative strategies of transforming Africa.

§ 5 §

FROM RECOVERY TO TRANSFORMATION?

The liberal-democratic model proffers a vision of 'capitalism with a human face'. Political and economic reform is expected not only to revive stagnant economies, but also to foster equity, satisfy basic needs, be environmentally sustainable, promote decentralization, and nurture popular sovereignty. Unfortunately, the programme promises more than it can deliver.

As people become disillusioned, they will probably show renewed interest in the ideas of radical intellectuals and social movements. The pendulum, now swinging so strongly toward liberal-democratic, free-market solutions, may later swing back as many of their fulsome promises remain unfulfilled. How desirable and politically feasible are the radical alternative models?

Despite the shortcomings of existing socialism identified in Chapter 2, Marxist theories have retained their appeal to many African intellectuals. These theories still offer a powerful critique of capitalism as it has evolved in Africa, and an invigorating vision of a participatory, classless, and non-exploitative future society. However, the rethinking of the flawed strategy of transition from the degraded dependent-capitalist society to the future socialist one is still limited. The key question remains unanswered: how will socialist movements avoid authoritarianism and inefficiency in the socialist transition?

Marxism retains much of its intellectual appeal as a holistic framework for understanding the defects and crises of capitalism in Africa.[1] For those who live in the midst of economic stagnation, mass poverty, marked inequalities, political oppression, widespread corruption, and foreign economic domination, faith in capitalist remedies runs against the grain. Colonialism, a recent event, is associated with capitalist expansion. Imperialism, in the forms of foreign economic influence and political manipulation, is experienced as humiliating and exploitative. Models premissed on the logic of global capitalist accumulation credibly explain the extreme vulnerability of Africa's highly dependent primary-export economies.[2] Associated class models make sense of the factional and self-serving behaviour of ascendant elites, as well as reassuring adherents by identifying the potential agents of social transformation, namely the workers and/or peasants.

Socialist theories focus upon the defects of the current conjuncture; they also offer hope for the future. Even with structural adjustment and an expanded inflow of official development assistance, the World Bank can offer Africa in the 1990s only modest improvements in economic indicators – together with a marked increase in the absolute numbers of poor people. In contrast, socialists envision a restructuring of economy and society that would permit ordinary people to satisfy their basic needs as well as gain greater control over their lives. Collective ownership of the means of production, cooperative production, and citizen participation in decision-making would, if achieved, create a more even distribution of economic and political power than that envisaged in the liberal-democratic model.

This egalitarian, participatory strand of the socialist vision is not just a pious hope; it has actually guided practice for brief periods in some of Africa's socialist revolutions. In Mozambique, for example, Frelimo fostered the active participation of people in villages and enterprises in the liberated zones in the two northern provinces before 1975. In September 1974 as Portuguese colonial authority disintegrated, Frelimo leader Samora Machel called for Grupos Dinamizadores (dynamizing groups) to establish themselves throughout the country. They sprang up, largely spontaneously, in villages, neighbourhoods in towns and cities, and workplaces. At independence in 1975 Frelimo extended this system of participatory democracy to the entire country. The dynamizing groups restored order, ran services, and kept enterprises operating amidst the chaos occasioned by the exodus of Portuguese technicians, administrators, and businessmen. The initial idea was that the people, mobilized in Grupos Dinamizadores and later Peoples' Assemblies, would complement the single party in control of the state.

This participatory approach was effectively replaced by a Leninist, top-down, centrally planned strategy at the party's Third Party Congress in 1977. Frelimo was to be a vanguard party. 'Democratic centralism' would prevail – that is, the party's top leadership would make all policy decisions. Party cells composed of members holding accepted Marxist–Leninist views would replace dynamizing groups. A hierarchy of peoples' assemblies would allow delegates to explain programmes to their electorates at the local level, and win the people's active support. Frelimo was to create mass organizations for workers, youth, women, journalists, and teachers; but, lacking autonomy from the vanguard party, these organizations could not fulfil the congress' grandiose admonition to serve as 'a school of democratic life and organised participation by the People...' (quoted in Egero 1987: 111). The Third Party Congress also decided to assign priority to the large state farms which had been established on former Portuguese settler holdings. The newly established communal villages and independent peasants were soon starved of resources.

Predictably, this Leninist approach, though pleasing to Mozambique's Soviet and Eastern European sponsors, smothered the democratic tendency. By the time of the second elections to the local-level Peoples' Assemblies in 1980, popular enthusiasm had already waned. Fewer people turned out to vote than in 1977 (Egero 1987: 125). Vanguardism and central planning had vitiated the power and functions of the assemblies, as all could see. A promising participatory experiment collapsed into a replica of Soviet-style bureaucratic collectivism. Only if the central leadership had made participatory democracy its highest priority could democratic institutions have flourished in a society lacking a democratic tradition.

A similar trajectory characterized the early years of the Ethiopian revolution. With the abolition of the landed estates in 1975, the revolutionary military government established peasant associations (*gebrewotch mahber*) as an agency of local self-administration. They catered for the peasants living within an area of 800 hectares or more – usually 150–300 households. An assembly of all members elected a chairman and an executive committee which handled day-to-day matters, and a judicial tribunal which adjudicated minor disputes. The associations initially had the important tasks of allocating land within their areas, especially that seized from the landlords, and maintaining law and order. Later, the government added less popular responsibilities. The associations organized the amalgamation of the scattered farming households into designated villages, collected taxes and extracted grain quotas from members at controlled prices. *Kebelles*, or dwellers' associations, were the counterpart of these associations in the towns and cities. The government created them when it abolished privately rented housing in 1975. Their primary task was to allocate housing and collect rents. Later, *kebelles* also distributed ration cards, ran cooperative shops, mounted literacy campaigns, adjudicated minor offences, and administered vigilante patrols of their neighbourhoods.

Both the peasant associations and the *kebelles* operated autonomously from 1975 to the end of the 'terror' in 1978, an autonomy buttressed by their roots in traditional forms of self-help associations (Salole 1991). The *gebrewotch mahber* rested on the tradition of community responsibility among the Amhara peasantry. The *kebelles* built their support upon the institution of the *edir*, which originated as a burial society. Even before the revolution, however, people had used the term to refer to all urban self-help voluntary associations. Over half the population of Addis Ababa belonged to an *edir* in the mid-1970s (Salole 1991: 9). After 1975, *kebelles* took over many of the functions formerly handled by the *edirs*, though the latter never disappeared. *Kebelles* even survived the overthrow of Colonel Mengistu's regime in May 1991; the new leaders reconstituted them under new leadership.

These indigenous self-help associations represented an incipient, but ultimately unrealized, institutional basis for a genuine, bottom-up participation. From 1978 to the liberalizing reforms of 1990, the Marxist–Leninist government moulded both sets of associations into agents of the party/state. Though elections continued at the base level, both institutions were organized into hierarchies controlled by the regional administration and officials of the Workers Party of Ethiopia. This party operated as a typical vanguard from its birth in 1984 until its death (along with official Marxism–Leninism) in 1990. Mass organizations other than the peasants' associations and *kebelles* also functioned as transmission belts for the party (Clapham 1989: 5–17).

Although the realities of socialism in power have blighted the socialist vision, the glorious moments of people's power inspire hope. Could not, in future transitions, the democratic tendency be accentuated to check the bureaucratic/oligarchical one?

The strategy of socialist transition has always been the Achilles heel of socialism. In practice, the economic strategy of modernization and industrialization via central planning has taken precedence over the political strategy of democratic mobilization. Top-down bureaucratic approaches require concentration of power and resources at the centre, hierarchy, restrictions on dissent, and privileges to technocratic elites. Where is the autonomous power to check oligarchical tendencies in this situation? Working-class and other mass organizations are creations of the vanguard group; the peasantry is too scattered and parochial to offer organized resistance. The survival of democratic tendencies therefore depends on the central leadership's commitment to mass participation; however, even a dedicated leadership will judge the slow processes of genuine participation an unendurable hindrance to its dealing effectively with urgent problems. Unchecked, the party/state apparatus will decline into authoritarianism and inefficiency.

Africa's socialists have responded to this manifest crisis of socialist theory and practice in three ways. One is a non-response: to persevere with traditional Leninist formulations of socialist strategy. Another is to advocate an intermediate 'national-popular' or 'national-democratic' path as a step towards an eventual socialist transition. A third approach is to urge socialists to join existing movements pressing for political as well as economic liberalization. Political liberalization, these thinkers expect, will allow socialists the time and the political space to build a socialist movement and devise a plausible democratic-socialist strategy. Each of these responses and nonresponses encounters its own set of difficulties.

First, some thinkers and political leaders persist with the traditional formulations of the appropriate socialist path. A book published by a prolific Nigerian Marxist economist in 1988 illustrates this intellectual tendency. Socialism, for Bade Onimode, is an historical necessity: '[j]ust as the capitalist mode of production and social formation succeeded its feudal predecessor, so the socialist transitional phase and social formation is the logical, higher level of development into which capitalism is transformed' (Onimode 1988: 40). His line of analysis is as follows. The source of Africa's underdevelopment is imperialism/neo-colonialism and its associated comprador classes in Africa. To overcome underdevelopment, socialist movements must organize and undertake class struggle.

This requires 'systematic mass mobilization', 'workers' control of enterprises', 'a vanguard party', and a 'scientific socialist ideology' (Onimode 1988: 271). In this struggle, the 'Marxist–Leninist party' will play a vanguard role. Its task is 'to design the programme of the class alliance, the general socialist strategy and give guidelines to the mass organizations'. As well, the vanguard must protect the trade unions, peasant associations, professional associations, and other mass organizations from 'petit-bourgeois influences' and carry out political education among their members (Onimode 1988: 314–15).

This formulation actually prescribes the same old bureaucratized and autocratic socialism that has already been found wanting. Not only is the desirability of this model questionable, but its practicability is dubious. How is the vanguard party to withstand the hostility of the local dispossessed propertied classes, the dominant capitalist powers, and the international financial institutions?

President Robert Mugabe and a section of the Zimbabwe African National Union (ZANU) also appeared to be oblivious to the evident pitfalls in affirming their commitment to a single-party state, a Leninist-type vanguardism, and a state-controlled economy for Zimbabwe in the 1980s. However, Mugabe was unable to carry the Central Committee of ZANU with him on this issue. In 1991 the government ended a decade of uncertainty when it announced a wideranging programme of economic liberalization.

A second response to the socialist crisis is to advocate a preparatory or intermediate stage between neo-colonialism (or 'bourgeois hegemony') and socialist transition (or 'proletarian hegemony'). Samir Amin, one of the continent's prominent Marxist intellectuals, argues that class relations and widespread poverty in the periphery sabotage both 'bourgeois democratic' and socialist strategies. Hence, he proposes a temporary middle way, a 'popular nationalist' project supported by a broad coalition of social forces and dedicated to delinking African economies from global capitalism in order to achieve greater self-reliance (Amin 1987: 1129–56). The prominent Tanzanian intellectual Issa Shivji similarly advocates a 'National Democratic revolution' involving the installation of a 'people's government' supported by an alliance of workers, peasants, and the anti-imperialist sections of the national bourgeoisie and petty bourgeoisie. The system would be democratic, though not *liberal*-democratic: 'as an ideology of resistance and struggle, democracy can only be cast in terms of *popular democracy* whose exact contours and forms of existence can only be determined in actual social struggles in given concrete, historical conditions' (Shivji 1991: 82). Only the large-scale private property in the hands of the imperialist and compradors would be expropriated. Small-scale private property and individual peasant production would remain (Shivji 1988).

Two recent popular-national experiments in West Africa exemplify the pitfalls of this vaguely defined route. Coups carried out by charismatic young military officers introduced both experiments: Flight-Lieutenant Jerry Rawlings in Ghana in December 1981, and Captain Thomas Sankara in Upper Volta (since renamed Burkina Faso) in August 1983. Both leaders appealed directly to 'the people', and articulated vague and moralistic ideologies which identified corrupt, self-serving elites and imperialism as the roots of their countries' economic and political malaise. Neither leader forged a cohesive movement or party that could weld together the disparate social forces to which he appealed. Instead, both populist regimes emphasized the importance of the direct and unmediated participation of the people through committees established in their workplaces and neighbourhoods. Despite the leaders' apparent sincerity and incorruptibility, their amorphous radicalism together with their movements' organizational fluidity soon sabotaged these experiments.

In Ghana, the revolutionary programme of the Provisional National Defence Council (PNDC) in 1982–3 indicated a popular-nationalist, though not Marxist–Leninist, orientation. Rawlings and his allies neither abolished private property nor founded a vanguard party. It was the corruption and inability of the elected Limann government to deal with the country's persistent economic decline that had instigated the coup. Thus, the new regime attacked 'retrogressive social forces' and 'imperialism', and announced 'power to the people', 'participatory democracy', and 'popular justice' (Rothchild and Gyimah-Boadi 1989: 222). It decreed price, rent, and transport fare controls. Militant elements of the army, police, and people's defence committee harassed traders suspected of hoarding goods. The government created 'people's' and cooperative farms to employ idle urban youth and spur agricultural production. All of these rhetorical flourishes and actions appealed to Rawlings' initial supporters: the radical intellectuals organized in a variety of small

leftist parties, the university students, the junior officers and en-
listed men, the urban workers and trade unions, and the urban
unemployed and poor.

The defence committee represented the prime channel of popular
participation in politics. Rawlings, in announcing the coup in December 1981, had called on the people to form committees to defend
the revolution. Hundreds of People's Defence Committee (PDCs)
sprung up in neighbourhoods and villages, and Workers' Defence
Committees (WDCs) emerged in workplaces. They were complemented by Citizens' Vetting Committees and Special Military Tri-
bunals to investigate and try cases of tax fraud and corruption.

But the regime erred in defining neither the functions nor the
membership of the defence committees in the early days. The result
was disorder and conflict:

the defence committees became battlegrounds for different political tendencies, being penetrated by 'reactionaries' and 'opportunists' (chiefs, one-
time politicians, traders) as well as by revolutionaries whose objectives
differed from those of the regime. The circumstances of their birth also led
the committees to indulge in the sterile exercise of popular power and
eclectic forms of struggle, such as harassment of petty traders, tiresome
checks on the population, instances of corruption and extortion, and
confrontations between rival defence committees over purely parochial
issues. (Hutchful 1986: 819)

Buffeted by the disorder occasioned partly by its own policies,
the government changed course in 1983. Although Rawlings had
inherited an economic crisis in 1981, he was faced with economic
chaos by 1983. This was partly a consequence of drought, bush fires,
and the repatriation of up to a million Ghanaians from Nigeria. It
also resulted from the regime's intimidation of traders, businessmen, and professionals, the hostility of the international financial
institutions, the disorder of the defence committees, and impractical
economic controls and pricing policies decreed by the government.
Although populist rhetoric continued, Rawlings sought to avert
economic collapse through a *rapprochement* with the International
Monetary Fund and locally powerful groups (Rothchild and Gyimah-Boadi 1989: 242). Radicals were purged from the PNDC and
other political bodies. The government abolished the PDCs and
WDCs in 1984, replacing them with Committees for the Defence of
the Revolution (CDRs). The CDRs were placed firmly under state
control, and assigned mainly economic tasks. Technocrats and

professional managers regained their authority within the public corporations. And the government began to show interest in the IMF's conventional policies for economic recovery: demand management, a growing reliance on market forces, and a restructuring and downsizing of the public sector. To reassure the middle classes, Justice D.F. Anan and traditional chiefs were appointed to the PNDC.

If, under the circumstances, the Rawlings regime has had no choice but to jettison its statist-populist policies, it has not shaped an organized coalition to support the new liberal direction. Rawlings has managed to survive several plots and coup attempts. But his regime remains vulnerable, having alienated its original urban supporters. It retains it popularity in the armed forces, especially among the disproportionately large contingent of Ewe soldiers. Farmers, especially cocoa producers, can be expected to favour the regime owing to its favourable pricing policies and its rehabilitation of the rural infrastructure (Crook 1990: 31–2). However, this rural support is not easily mobilized, whereas most urban groups are indifferent or hostile to the government. Decentralization in the form of the elected District Assemblies created in 1988 has gone some way in restoring popular participation.

Long-term stability requires that the regime abandon its hallmark organizational fluidity and suspicion of political parties in favour of a system of representative democracy. Such groups as the middle-class Movement for Freedom and Justice and Ghana Bar Association, the radical Kwame Nkrumah Revolutionary Guards and National Union of Ghanaian Students, and the Trade Union Congress vociferously demanded multiparty democracy in 1990–1. In May 1991, the PNDC bowed to the pressure by announcing its acceptance in principle of multiparty politics. However, while the government-appointed National Commission for Democracy prepared a draft constitution for a national referendum, the ban on parties would continue.

Burkina Faso has followed a similar trajectory, except that the murder of the populist leader and his close associates preceded the change in direction. The 'popular-democratic' phase opened with the *coup d'état* of August 1983 which brought the Conseil National de la Révolution (CNR) to power under the leadership of Captain Thomas Sankara. It closed four years later with the assassination of

Sankara by his supposed friend and colleague, Captain Blaise Compaoré.

Sankara declared *la Révolution Burkinabè* to be 'popular' and 'democratic', rather than socialist (Martin 1986). It involved, he claimed, the transfer of power from the bourgeoisie to *le Peuple* – an alliance of the working class, the petty bourgeoisie, the peasantry, and the lumpenproletariat. The people were to exercise their power through two political organizations: the CNR (in charge of national planning and direction), and the Comités de Défense de la Révolution (CDRs). The latter, as the 'authentic' instrument of popular power, would deter counterrevolution, raise popular consciousness, and organize collective and voluntary work. In the economic sphere, the popular-democratic revolution entailed, not collective ownership, but the construction of an independent, self-reliant, and planned economy oriented to the satisfaction of basic human needs.

The 'Popular-Democratic Revolution' was more than merely high-flown rhetoric. It was 'popular' in the sense that the leadership enforced austerity and honesty in the higher levels of the armed forces and civil service, while transferring income from this hitherto influential urban elite to the peasantry. The modest Renault 5 replaced the Mercedes-Benz as the official car of high-level officials. A salary freeze, a diminution of the perquisites of rank, an involuntary saving scheme, and increases in the controlled price of foodstuffs all reduced the purchasing power of the bureaucratic and military elite. The peasants were the main beneficiaries: they not only received higher returns on agricultural commodities, but also benefited from government assistance in the construction of wells, schools, health clinics, and schemes to combat soil erosion in this fragile Sahelian region. It was clear to the impoverished rural majority that the government in Ouagadougou was sympathetic and determined to assist their self-help activities (Harsch 1988b: 36).

Although Sankara took popular participation seriously, the revolution was always a largely top-down affair (Martin 1989). The CNR remained under the control of a coalition of young, left-wing officers. Ministers in the government were drawn from this coalition, as well as the various small parties of the left which preoccupied the middle class and trade unions in Ouagadougou. The CDRs were never authentic organs of people's power, except at the grassroots level. At the base – in towns, villages, schools, universities, and military and paramilitary units – the CDRs operated fairly autonomously in dealing with local matters. Opportunistic and irresponsible elements seized control of some CDRs, and used them to persecute their enemies and advance their own interests. In the villages, it was not unusual for chiefs to control the CDRs. The people were never permitted to debate the policy directions adopted by the CNR; this central power controlled the CDRs at the departmental, provincial, and national levels. This vitiated debate in the Comités Departementaux, Pouvoirs Révolutionaires Provinciaux, and Congrès des CDRs. The CNR also established mass organizations for women, youth, the old, and the peasants; however, these had not yet evolved into autonomous bodies at the time of Compaoré's coup.

The murder of Sankara and subsequent change of policy direction illustrate the vulnerability of national-popular experiments led by army officers. Although Compaoré has claimed that Sankara's intention to execute Compaoré and his associates precipitated the coup of October 1987, he has never revealed any evidence to support this allegation. It appears that Compaoré and his co-conspirators moved to pre-empt what they saw as a bid by Sankara to centralize power in his own hands. Sankara had planned to group all the leftist parties into a single ruling front, and to forge an elite military unit under his personal command. Whatever the motives, the coup permitted Compaoré to retain the revolution's populist rhetoric while jettisoning its content under the banner of 'Rectification'. The urban-based elite assumed their former privileged position at the expense of the rural masses. Compaoré returned to the 'traditional' alliance of urban bureaucratic and military elites with traditional and religious leaders; terminated the CDRs; and built a hierarchical and secretive regime which soon consumed the new leader's co-conspirators in the 1987 coup.

In 1991, Compaoré engineered a transition to multiparty elections that seemed designed to ensure his own election as president. The new constitution, approved by a June referendum, barred the military from holding office. Captain Compaoré thus resigned his commission, though opposition parties claimed that the former officer still used state resources to win support for his candidacy. The opposition demanded that Compaoré permit a broadly representative 'national conference' to design a constitution and oversee the subsequent elections. He refused. The opposition then successfully boycotted the election of December 1991. Compaoré's efforts to manipulate 'democratization' had failed.

Rawlings' and Sankara's popular-national 'revolutions' were both sincere attempts to achieve social justice, probity in office, popular participation, and greater self-reliance. But good intentions are not enough. Libya's national-populist Colonel Gaddafhi has survived while calling (though not providing) for power to the people because of the leader's ruthlessness and access to oil riches. Neither Rawlings nor Sankara, however, commanded the same ruthlessness or resources. They alienated foreign and local elites without building a strong alternative base and development strategy. Although their efforts to channel benefits to the rural poor were laudatory, peasants are a notoriously weak political base. Lacking an organizational means of channelling popular support and obtaining legitimacy, both radical regimes remained highly vulnerable to challengers. The economic crisis, magnified by the inept policies and radical rhetoric, compounded their problems.

In sum, popular-national alternatives, even if animated by commendable intentions, risk disaster and reversal unless their organizational, ideological, and policy weaknesses are rectified.

A third response to the crisis of socialist theory and practice is temporarily to set aside the socialist project in order to take advantage of the present conjuncture. Claude Ake, for instance, accepts that African development policy is firmly set on an IMF-backed course of economic liberalization. 'The battalions have marched out to liberate the market, already we hear the din of battle,' he observes. Ake enjoins socialists to put their energies into advancing political rights by employing liberal rhetoric. 'What we can do is to extend the battle, extend the liberalization of the economy to politics and society, and bring to everyone's attention the costly contradictions of capitalism dissociated from its political correlates of liberalism,' he explains (Ake 1990: 591).

Why should socialists set aside their longstanding distrust of 'bourgeois' democracy in order to become its supporters? On the one hand, third-world liberal democracies have generally made only limited progress in mitigating the inequalities, poverty, and injustice in their societies. 'Democracy', as many Marxists contend, is a potent component of a hegemonic ideology that legitimates, and thus perpetuates, these inegalitarian social orders. On the other hand, the instrumental Leninist view that liberal democracy is a sham, simply the political superstructure of competitive capitalism, is simplistic. To the extent that liberal democracy protects some civil and political rights of all citizens, it is valuable to all. It is certainly valuable to the publicized middle-class victims of human rights violations – intellectuals, university students, journalists, and professionals. But it also provides some means of defence to the 'invisible' day-to-day victims. Workers, traders, and peasants are most subject to daily intimidation, shake-downs, and the caprice of soldiers and the police, not the 'big man' in the Mercedes.

A functioning capitalist democracy also affords progressive forces the political space to survive, rethink socialist strategy, and, within limits, organize. Liberal democracy is thus a 'double edged sword' (Cunningham 1987: 158–9). Although its institutions are historically associated with capitalism and facilitate the latter's reproduction, its political and civil liberties and parliamentary institutions are also available to its opponents – those who aim to wring concessions from the dominant classes and supersede liberal democracy by extending democratic procedures from the political into the economic sphere.

However, if liberal democracy permits socialists to continue their political work, it also presents them with difficult strategic choices. 'How can a popular movement strengthen democracy so as to avoid another collapse into military rule, while simultaneously challenging the exclusionary mechanisms of specific democratic institutions' (Barros 1986: 64)? This question, which has provoked much debate in Latin America, is now relevant to African countries as they undergo some measure of political liberalization. The dilemma is acute. Socialists may reassure suspicious elites by accepting narrow limits on social reforms; but they will also invite popular disillusion with an ineffectual socialist movement. On the other hand, if socialist movements press against these limits by mobilizing mass support behind a radical programme of redistribution and extended democracy, they will signal to the dominant groups that democracy is getting out of hand. A coup then becomes probable.

Some socialists will doubt that the benefits of bourgeois democracy warrant these restrictions and frustrations. But, in light of the limited rethinking of social transition strategies, the tactical embrace of political liberalization seems the best socialist option in countries not irredeemably mired in tyranny and disorder. In the latter cases, revolution – with all its costs and uncertainties – may afford the only hope for a better life. In most countries, however, the external and domestic pressures for liberalization favour some measure of formal democratization.

Disillusioned or disheartened by socialism in practice, wary of authoritarian populism, and unpersuaded by the claims of democratic capitalism, many thinkers have sought refuge in the vague but progressive notions of 'human' or 'people-centred' development. In the prosperous seventies, progressive economists, foundations, and agencies rejected top-down, growth-fixated, authoritarian, and environmentally damaging patterns of development. They opted for a radical alternative model – variously labelled 'another development', 'basic-needs development', 'ecodevelopment', and 'participatory development' (e.g., Dag Hammarskjold Foundation 1975; International Labour Organization 1976; Grant 1981; Sandbrook 1982: ch. 1). Emergency measures occasioned by the severe economic crisis of the 1980s swept these unconventional models aside. Structural adjustment, first in the IMF's form of demand management to achieve financial equilibrium, and later in the more sophisticated form of the World Bank's growth-oriented adjustment, became the order of the day. But the limited economic success of structural adjustment, the human costs of this process, and the dismal projections of Africa's future have renewed interest in 'another development'.

Although specific formulations vary, all the alternative approaches share these basic principles. They aim to promote a pattern of economic growth which is both oriented to the satisfaction of basic human needs and ecologically sustainable. Since domestic and global production and power structures allegedly obstruct the realization of a basic-needs strategy, popular empowerment is a precondition of this strategy as well as an important goal in itself. Only if people participate in making the decisions that affect their lives will these decisions advance the interests of the poor majority, activate popular enthusiasm, and take account of the precise economic realities throughout the country. These programmes also universally emphasize the virtues of self-reliance and of building on endogenous skills and resources. This is not, however, a prescription for autarchy: 'collective self-reliance' on a regional basis as well as continued international economic linkages will complement the promotion of local and national self-reliance in food, other necessities, and technological development.

Recent formulations of 'human-' or 'people-centred' development emphasize a new element – the developmental role of civil society (Korten 1990; Clark 1991). Earlier models of basic-needs approaches assumed that the state, albeit democratized, would be the prime mover. In the meantime, however, Africans and Latin Americans have had to fend for themselves as states failed as instruments of 'development'. Social movements also demonstrated their potential power in the 1980s; they forced significant political and economic changes in Eastern Europe, Latin America, Philippines, and South Africa. Now, people-centred development portrays peoples' and voluntary organizations[3] as playing an active role in mobilizing public support and building more self-reliant societies.

Economists and intergovernmental agencies have dominated the formulation of basic-needs approaches; consequently, the *politics* of basic needs has received short shrift (Sandbrook 1982). Clearly, the models advocate changes which together constitute a socio-economic transformation. Most assume, for instance, an initial redistribution of assets, especially land, in order to underpin a pattern of basic-needs-oriented growth. But proponents of these approaches dodge the crucial question of whether private or some form of collective ownership will be needed. Some formulations give the impression that a radically reformed capitalism is feasible. Others evoke or assume a refurbished socialist system which is true to its libertarian vision. This lack of ideological clarity is not necessarily a disadvantage in the early stages: it allows people sharing a 'bottom-up', self-reliant approach to cooperate in an open-ended process of self-empowerment. However, any speculation on the feasibility of human-centred development cannot avoid the fundamental ideological and political questions.

The United Nations' Economic Commission for Africa (ECA) champions a needs-oriented, self-reliant, participatory, and (more recently) environmentally protective development strategy for African countries. Although the World Bank has borrowed some of the rhetoric of human-centred development since 1989 (see World Bank 1989a), the ECA nonetheless advocates far more radical change than that envisaged by the international financial institutions.

The Lagos Plan of Action, which was adopted by the Assembly of Heads of State and Government of the Organization of African Unity (OAU) in April 1980, forcefully stated the ECA's ambitious early programme for Africa's transformation. In essence, Africa had to replace its export-led development model with a more inward-looking, self-reliant thrust. Africa must use its extensive resources primarily for its own development. Although economies would continue to produce primary commodities for traditional export markets, they would progressively achieve greater self-sufficiency in food and manufacturing production. Collective self-reliance was the goal; sub-regional common markets would develop and lay the groundwork for a continent-wide African Economic Community by the year 2000. Africans would thereby break their excessive dependency on Western markets, investment, and technical expertise, though without striving for autarchy. Producers would realize economies of scale in the expanded markets. Countries would share and augment their limited technical talent.

Unfortunately, however, the African governments who endorsed the Lagos Plan largely ignored their policy commitments in the 1980s.

Hence, in 1989 the Economic Commission for Africa reformulated some of the earlier ideas in an 'African Alternative Framework' to conventional structural adjustment programmes (UNECA 1989). Whereas the World Bank advocates opening up African economies to global market forces, the ECA contends that it is largely the external dependency of these mono-cultural economies that accounts for their lack of dynamism. For reasons enumerated later, it argues that betting Africa's future on the global economy is highly problematical. Some countries adopting structural adjustment programmes may register gains in conventional performance indicators, such as gross domestic product, export growth, balance of payments, and budgetary balances. Yet, an ECA report notes, these countries will still not have progressed in realizing Africa's central objectives – poverty alleviation, sustainable growth, and food self-sufficiency (UNECA 1989: 25).

Hence, the ECA again stresses the importance of diversification away from dependence on one or several commodity exports, and of national and collective self-reliance. Goals should include food self-sufficiency, the harmonization of investment plans and tariffs within sub-regional markets to prevent duplication of industries and expand intra-African trade, the transformation of consumer preferences from Western-derived foods and other goods to those produced locally, and the development of appropriate products and technologies. The 'endogenisation of development' would require regional cooperation not just in trade, but in technological innovation and investment as well (UNECA 1989: 13).

The Commission also implicitly proposes a larger role for the state in Africa's economic life than does the IMF or World Bank. The socio-economic transformations it advocates will not eventuate without strong political leadership and coherent development strategies. It champions '[a] judicious mix between expanded private initiatives and efficient government intervention ... to create an environment that would enable both the private and public sectors to thrive ...'. With their many responsibilities in promoting production, governments 'would need to yield to the private sector only progressively' (UNECA 1989: 47).

But can the state today play this developmental role? The ECA's report recognizes the prevalent weaknesses of African public sectors: poor management, inefficiency, corruption and destructive political conflict. Popular participation features as the chief remedy. Accountable, democratic governments are more disciplined and responsive to the needs of the people than authoritarian ones. The ECA's alternative model

calls for greater accountability and dedicated and patriotic management on the part of the public sector. At the institutional level, there is need for excessively centralized bureaucracies to yield to local decentralization, grass-roots initiatives and community self-management... The increased role of the people in adjustment with transformation should facilitate the functioning of a system of checks and balances and safe-guard against bureaucratic excesses. (UNECA 1989: 47)

Despite the ECA's stress on socio-economic transformation and its awareness of the centrality of political power, the 'alternative framework' constitutes largely a technocratic exercise – and unfortunately an occasionally obscure one at that. There are only scattered references to national and international power relations and occasional exhortations to governments to democratize. As an agency of the United Nations, the Economic Commission for Africa must obviously tread wearily in a context where many of the member-states of the OAU are still autocratically governed. None-theless, its avoidance of any analysis of the political agents of struc-tural transformation significantly diminishes the credibility of its alternative.

Perhaps in recognition of this, the ECA deepened its commitment to participatory, people-centred development by convening an 'In-ternational Conference on Popular Participation in the Recovery and Development Process in Africa' in Arusha, Tanzania in Febru-ary 1990. The populist tenor of the meeting was symbolically af-firmed by the central location accorded to people's organizations in the conference hall. The Commission's then Executive Secretary, Dr Adebayo Adedeji, set the tone in his opening remarks:

[T]he foundation for self-reliant and internally self-sustaining processes of development is people's participation. It is the engine for launching the processes for economic transformation. It is the motor for accelerating the process of change and development. For development is not merely a transformation of the structures and material attributes of a society. Au-thentic, self-reliant processes of development inevitably result in the trans-formation of the people who bring about the change. (Adedeji 1990: 4)

The 'African Charter for Popular Participation in Development and Transformation', adopted at the Arusha conference and later endorsed by the heads of state of the OAU, duly reflected these views (UNECA 1990). It speaks of 'empowerment of the people' as a crucial means and end of 'human-centred development'. And it enjoins people's organizations to assert their autonomy, develop their internal democratic procedures, and press for democratic par-ticipation at all levels of decision-making.

How desirable and feasible is the ECA's radical alternative to the liberal-democratic, free-enterprise approach? Economists would raise legitimate technical objections to some of the specific analyses, projections, and prescriptions of the alternative framework. This evaluation, however, focuses only upon its broad direction of equi-table, participatory and self-reliant development, a programme ad-vocated by many social movements and intellectuals throughout the world (Korten 1990). I will suggest that human-centred develop-ment, though admirable in principle, lacks a plausible political strategy to achieve its recommended socio-economic transform-ation. This strategy therefore represents a risky gamble in the 1990s.

It will take many years for the radical democratic movements and developmental states that must underpin this transformation to mature. However, some less controversial elements of the approach, in particular the promotion of intra-African trade and cooperation, are of immediate relevance.

One strength of the ECA's model is its recognition that poor people in sub-Saharan countries are unlikely to prosper on the basis of conventional, export-led growth. According to the World Bank's projections, this strategy will not relieve poverty in these countries by the year 2000 even under favourable growth assumptions. Even if this region succeeds in achieving a growth rate of 4 per cent per annum in the 1990s (which now appears unlikely), the poor will still grow from 180 million in 1985 to 265 million by the end of the century (World Bank 1990a). The bleak prospect for sustained growth flows mainly from the weak international demand for Africa's primary commodities. Their prices are unlikely to recover much from their depressed levels in the 1980s, despite short-term fluctuations. Sluggish growth and persistent protectionism in the industrial North, synthetic substitutes, and new technologies requiring less or different raw-material inputs weaken demand for Africa's traditional exports. And the proliferation of new Asian and Latin American competitors in commodity markets augments global supply.

Africa's dependence on the North for crucial factors of production compounds the region's problems. Financial inflows are inadequate because commercial banks are unwilling to lend to the heavily indebted sub-Saharan countries, foreign investors have not yet been enticed by more attractive business environments, and aid has recently stagnated in real terms. If repayments and interest are deducted from disbursements of new loans from all sources, then net inflows to sub-Saharan Africa are either negative (as in 1985) or low (only a projected $US657 in 1990) (World Bank 1990c: 130–3). The net flow of foreign direct investment into sub-Saharan Africa in the 1980s totalled only $US200–300 million annually. Yet, according to the International Finance Corporation of the World Bank, sustained economic growth required a ten-fold increase, to $US3 billion each year (Morna 1991: 42). Africa's reliance upon foreign experts also creates several well-known problems. The foreigners rarely transfer their expertise to African counterparts;

their unfamiliarity with the local culture and political environment inhibits informed decision-making; and they are often biased in favour of Western techniques and practices whose appropriateness to capital- and skill-scarce and labour-rich Africa is questionable.

In light of these harsh economic realities, a collectively self-reliant and needs-oriented development path seems to offer more hope for future broad-based prosperity than the conventional approach. Africa is being progressively marginalized within the global economy as its share of world trade shrinks and its technological base stagnates. The alternative model would, in principle, alter this trend. Africa would rely largely on its own resources and the ingenuity and energy of its people to produce goods mainly for the consumption of its own population in expanded common markets. The lack of a politics of transition, however, may render this option utopian.

Another attractive feature of people-centred development is its emphasis upon empowering people. Empowerment is a word that is often invoked but rarely defined. The Economic Commission for Africa and the World Bank, among others, use the term very loosely. Empowerment, for some, refers to a process by which a particular deprived or oppressed group (the poor, peasants, women, a caste, class or ethnic group) develop a sense of agency or efficacy. Others focus upon political action rather than psychological uplift; empowering people enables them to shape decision affecting their lives by expanding their autonomy, resources, and capability, and by democratizing institutions. Both the sense of agency and exercise of agency are important. Empowerment as psychological liberation is a valuable end in itself, and the political participation of marginalized groups may reorient states toward a more equitable and sustainable development.

In theory, self-esteem and confidence replace despair and hopelessness as poor or oppressed people participate in their own self-empowerment. Joining independent organizations, even those dedicated to such supposedly apolitical objectives as community self-help, is a principal means of self-empowerment. Isolated individuals or those who belong to corporatist bodies controlled by the state lack power. Experience in collective decision-making and leadership produce in people a sense of controlling their own destinies. Membership in autonomous social organizations may shape empowering social identities, as, for example, women belonging to their own organizations may come to question their subordination to men. To the extent that networks link individual associations – through church, mosque, or umbrella associations of peasant unions, trade unions, or community associations – the social power of members is magnified.

Empowerment is also a means to other ends. In the 1980s, African governments have generally dealt ineffectually with the massive problems of economic stagnation, absolute poverty, environmental degradation, and social violence. Only by strengthening civil society through collective self-empowerment can people (a) effectively tackle some of these pressing problems on their own, and (b) generate in governments the political will and mobilized support to attack the interrelated facets of the African crisis. On the one hand, people cannot realistically wait for their states to develop the will and capacities to deal with all these problems; people and their voluntary associations must often take the lead. People's and voluntary organizations are in a better position to mobilize popular talents, energies, and creativity than hierarchically organized, resource-starved, and demoralized governmental bureaucracies. Already, self-help grassroots associations in most sub-Saharan countries have lessened the passivity and the governmental dependency of their members. Village improvement associations have built and maintained schools, clinics, community centres, and safe communal water supplies. Revolving credit associations (*tontines* in francophone countries) have provided the credit without which small entrepreneurs cannot survive. Grassroots associations are also playing a major role in the continuing struggle against environmental degradation. They are, here and there, organizing the planting of trees or the construction of drainage basins and other defences against soil erosion. Owing to the massive scale on which this battle must be waged, grassroots participation is essential.

On the other hand, civil society cannot develop itself without the cooperation of government. Governments must at least permit people to help themselves. Empowerment, by enhancing the accountability, responsiveness, and capacity of the state, builds a basis for a fruitful collaboration between it and civil society.

However attractive the philosophy and objectives of human-centred development, its widespread implementation unfortunately remains a distant prospect. Consider the hurdles which the ECA's radical alternative must negotiate.

First, it is sobering how little progress Africa has made in implementing collective self-reliance. Since over half of Africa's countries have populations under 10 million, economic progress demands regional cooperation. Yet only about 6 per cent of Africa's officially recorded international trade takes place among African countries; the region remains as dependent upon commodity exports to the industrial world as ever (World Bank 1989a: 158). Governments have allowed interstate jealousies and suspicions to inhibit economic cooperation. The ideal of collective self-reliance is enshrined in several sub-regional organizations: the Economic Community of West African States (ECOWAS), La Communauté Economique de l'Afrique de l'Ouest (CEAO), L'Union Douanière et Economique de l'Afrique Centrale (UDEAC), the Preferential Trade Area (PTA), and the Southern African Development Coordination Conference (SADCC). Although these associations have made some progress, none has yet established common external tariffs or coordinated their members' investment plans.

The UDEAC, for example, emerged in 1964 on the ashes of the Union Douanière Equatoriale whose members were Congo, Chad, Central African Republic, Gabon, and Cameroon. The organization's goal were to adopt a common external tariff and common export and import duties, and promote free movement of goods, labour, and capital. Yet inter-state trade among the six members (Equatorial Guinea recently joined the five listed above) has not grown appreciably over the years, as each state has jealously guarded its own interests. There have, however, been some useful common projects, such as a common attack on endemic diseases and the creation of a sub-regional think-tank.

The Preferential Trade Area, formed in 1984, has made some progress towards a common market linking its eighteen members in eastern and southern Africa. In 1990, about 400 items were eligible for preferential tariffs. These included food and agricultural raw materials, as well as non-agricultural raw materials, intermediate and capital goods, and consumer durables and non-durables. A major impediment to trade among the members was that most lacked convertible currencies to settle their accounts, which came due every seventy-five days. The PTA has tried to mitigate this problem by creating a Unit of Account (similar in function to the IMF's Special Drawing Rights) to which the members' currencies are pegged.

SADCC, created in 1979 to lessen its members' dependence upon apartheid South Africa, is perhaps the most successful regional grouping in Tropical Africa. Its members are Angola, Botswana, Lesotho, Malawi, Mozambique, Namibia, Swaziland, Tanzania, Zambia, and Zimbabwe. Unlike the others, SADCC has concentrated on removing physical barriers to trade rather than on promoting free trade among its members. It has succeeded (with considerable support from foreign donors) in rehabilitating railway lines through Mozambique and Angola to the sea, and in improving telephone communications among its members. The organization's priority in the 1990s is to expand trade among its members to 12 per cent of the members' total international trade from its currently dismal 5 per cent (Morna 1990: 51–2).

Although the OAU has abandoned the goal of establishing an African Economic Community by the year 2000, it still intends to move ahead on a more realistic schedule. An OAU Heads of State meeting in Abuja, Nigeria in June 1991 approved a plan to create an African Economic Community by 2025. A phased transition will move from regional free trade zones and customs unions to a continental customs union, and by the year 2020 to an African common market as a precursor to a full-blown economic community. Perhaps the hard economic times in the 1990s and the paucity of external assistance will this time engender the will to follow through with this ambitious initiative. The road to a self-reliant Africa, as originally envisaged in the Lagos Plan, will be long and difficult. Yet, as one observer aptly observes, '[d]espite the paucity of implementation, the [Lagos] plan is not dead, nor is it likely to die, because it offers the only real hope for Africa to realize its potential' (Browne 1989: 408).

A second hurdle to human-centred development is governmental intransigence and/or incapacity. A shift towards self-sufficiency in foodstuffs and consumer goods will have to overcome the opposition of powerful urban groups wedded to current patterns of production, consumption, and export-orientation. Engineering collective self-reliance in technology, investment, and trade will require considerable expertise, diplomatic finesse, not to mention political will. Local self-reliance implies autonomous community organizations that central elites have normally suppressed as threatening to national integration and their own hold on power. Empowerment of the poorest and most oppressed groups – the landless, the urban unemployed, the seasonal and casual labourers, the hawkers and petty artisans, and women – is more threatening still. How are states, many of which are still weak and dominated by rent-seeking political insiders, to be reoriented and enabled to undertake their transformational role?

Democratization, according to the ECA and other proponents, will shape a more responsive and accountable state. Citizens will participate in the decisions that affect their lives at both the local and national levels. But how will this happen? Again one runs headlong into a vicious circle: a genuine democratic transition and consolidation requires the mobilization of a demanding civil society, yet how can the poor and marginal organize and participate in such a mobilization when they are often denied basic political rights and suffer from illiteracy, malnutrition, and disease? Privileged classes are unlikely to acquiesce in the restructuring of political institutions in ways that undermine their power and privileges. Even in liberal democracies, these classes have the means to protect their interests. So how will social movements rooted in the people force the changes? The ECA's technocratic orientation leaves the crucial political strategy unspecified.

The politics of structural transformation are daunting. Empowering people challenges power structures. In Kenya, for example, the government has treated with suspicion even the Green Belt Movement, an indigenous environmental group whose principal aim is to organize rural women to plant trees and conserve soil. When asked to explain this hostility, the movement's leader responded that her association threatens political leaders because it

is organizing ordinary people, poor people, and it is empowering them – telling them that they can cause positive change to their environment and that they can do it on their own. African governments do not encourage and have not yet accepted the fact that the people can direct their own destiny. They want to guide them and they want to be followed blindly. They do not want their people informed or organized because organized groups threaten their position. They know that if people are empowered and informed, they can be agents of change. (W. Maathai quoted in Topouzis 1990: 31)

The Kenyan government in 1991 felt sufficiently concerned about the activities of non-governmental organizations to establish a statutory board to monitor and regulate them.

Earlier attempts at 'bottom-up' development foundered largely for political and bureaucratic reasons. Cooperative societies to provide marketing and other services for small farmers, *animation rurale* in the former French colonies, and 'community development' at the village level were portrayed as a bottom-up approach when each came into vogue in the 1950s and 1960s. Yet none of these movements achieved the hoped-for results (Midgley *et al.* 1986). Rigid governmental bureaucracies converted each experiment into a vehicle for promoting government programmes. Bureaucrats were oriented towards the centralized provision of services. They were also used to giving commands and advice to villagers, not to responding to the expressed needs of self-confident and organized peasants. Even donor agencies and development NGOs, though paying lip-service to popular participation, were driven by the imperatives of 'moving money' and achieving targets to push village projects through with little community input into the definition of priorities or the design of projects (Gow and VanSant 1983: 429). As well, the locally powerful tended to dominate all the local institutions and to divert benefits from development projects to themselves. Or local factional rivalries divided the people, making cooperative, self-reliant development virtually impossible.

The more radical and systemic 'basic-needs' approaches of the 1970s suffered a similar fate. Whereas the community development movement has focused upon the uplift of isolated villages, these new approaches called for the transformation of entire societies of which the villages formed a part. Mass participation would fuel this transformation. But, in practice, development agencies and governments embraced the rhetoric while diluting the content. The politically challenging notion that national and global production and power structures perpetuate mass poverty was dropped. Instead of a systemic assault on poverty, the basic-needs approach became

a series of unrelated programmes for provision ... of water, food, shelter, health care, etc., sector by sector, population group by population group ... There is little chance that the 'sector' would come together in the more troubling form of 'self-reliance'; nor is it likely that the population groups being provided for would begin to see common interests among themselves (for example, among the rural and urban poor). (Wisner 1988: 89)

How can a people-centred development strategy overcome the intransigence of powerful interests? Governments will not adopt a participatory and needs-oriented approach simply because it accords with the long-term interests of their poor majorities. The success of such approaches will presumably depend, not upon benevolent governments, but upon an 'invisible' process of empowering the disempowered. Only strong social movements will possess the values and the social power to impel a responsive, democratic and capable state along the road to egalitarian development.

Yet the strengthening of civil associations, though crucial, is insufficient; it must be accompanied by the democratization of these associations. Lest we forget, some tyrannies and inequalities have their roots in civil society, not only in state structures and practices. Patriarchy, racism, ethnic chauvinism, and class domination are perpetuated in and by many civil associations. The current tendency to romanticize people's and voluntary organizations masks this unpleasant fact. The struggle for freedom and equality – for people-centred development – will therefore be waged within the arenas of civil society as well as the state.

In countries characterized until recently by authoritarian governments and weak civil societies, strengthening and democratizing peoples' and voluntary associations will take years. First, and most obviously, the process requires that civil associations install internal democratic procedures and root out discrimination and inequalities based upon gender, ethnicity, and status. This alone represents a major challenge.

Secondly, the process involves increasing the autonomy, density, and interactions of people's and voluntary organizations. A dense web of independent associations changes the political equation by easing the apathy and acquiescence on which authoritarian regimes thrive. Networking on a national, regional, and global scale among civil associations sharing common objectives is a potent means of building the social power of civil society. Networking allows organizations to share information, build solidarity on issues, promote joint or simultaneous action, and bring external publicity to bear on abuses of power or wrong-headed governmental policies in any member country. Technological advances in the form of rapid air transport, photocopying, and fax machines now facilitate networking on a regional and global scale. Moreover, networks have the advantage of resiliency – the cooptation of one or more members does not destroy the network.

Independent national associations of indigenous NGOs have

emerged recently in many African countries to advance common goals. The Nigerian Association of Voluntary Development Organizations (NAVDO), the Ghanaian Association of Private Organizations in Development (GAPVOD), the Conseil des organisations non-gouvernementales d'appui au développement (CONGAD) in Senegal, the Tanzanian Association of Non-Governmental Organizations (TANGO), and the recently formed Zambian NGOs Inter-Agency Working Group exemplify this networking trend. These umbrella organizations can, among other things, assist in the formation of grassroots people's organizations – smallholders' cooperative, consumer protection associations, women's self-improvement and protection associations, youth's skill-improvement clubs, etc. These grassroots organizations then, if the political situation permits, form coalitions at regional levels, at which representatives of the grassroots associations participate along with others from regional or national umbrella organizations. In future, continental and global associations may further enhance the social power of progressive forces.

Thirdly, buttressing the political face of civil society – the institutions which monitor abuse of power, punish the offenders, and articulate political demands – is crucial to empowerment. Independent newspapers, human-rights associations, interest groups, and political parties are some of the key organizations. As the previous chapter noted, recent years have seen a recrudescence of these intermediary associations. Human rights organizations, in particular, have flourished as African governments have come under pressure to liberalize. Some of these, such as Togo's National Commission on Human Rights, were established on a government's initiative. But many others, notably Nigeria's Civil Liberties Organization, Ghana's Association of Democratic Lawyers, and Zimbabwe's well-established Catholic Commission for Justice and Peace in Zimbabwe, have established a hardy independence from government. Demonstrations, political strikes, and rebellions register the demands and grievances of sections of civil society, and mobilize support against abuses of power.

Finally, fortifying the independent powers and resources of local governments will give impetus to bottom-up development. Central governments have generally dominated municipal governments in sub-Saharan countries. Although most local authorities still exercise only limited functions, suffer appointed or manipulated leaderships, and command negligible independent finances, the trend, as noted in Chapter 3, is towards greater devolution. This is a good thing, because, in principle, local government is a critical point of encounter between civil society and the state. Activists hope that

the new popular organisations, associations and cooperatives in the cities [will] provide new grass roots leadership which can mobilise votes, field independent councilmen ... and in this way make popular interests felt in local government, thereby forcing a more equitable redistribution of local public resources in favour of the poor. At the same time, it is hoped that a better and more stable democratic structure will evolve based on inter-mediate organisations and leadership controlled through grass roots par-ticipation, and hence more responsive to the interest of the poor majorities. (Wils 1988: 74)

Eventually, these new local-regional democratic structures may extend to the national level.

Would such a process of empowerment ultimately entail a social-ist transition, or is it compatible with a radically reformist capi-talism? This question, though rarely posed in discussions of people-centred development, must be confronted by movements working to advance 'bottom-up' transformation. Inasmuch as socialist theory and practice remain in crisis, socialism seems a risky option. No plausible strategies for avoiding the despotism and inefficiency of bureaucratic collectivism currently exist, as discussed earlier in this chapter.

Might then human-centred development be achieved by means of a radically reformist, national-popular path, and hence with the potential support of small-scale private business? The experience of national-populism in power in Ghana and Burkina Faso does not inspire confidence. As heartening as is the rhetorical emphasis upon participatory democracy and basic human needs, its moralistic and simplistic ideology, organizational fluidity, and dependence upon a charismatic leader constituted a fragile basis for a long-term, trans-formational strategy. A radical coup represents a particularly prob-lematic route to people-centred development when the charismatic leader attacks corruption and inequity by increasing state regu-lation. Only a popular-democratic movement which emerges from below, from a process of self-empowerment, can hope to sustain a people-centred development. And this seems to be a distant prospect.

'**Reform** may be a dirty word ... but it begins to look more and more like the most promising route to success in the real world. I limit myself to *most promising* rather than *only* for the simple reason that all certitude must now be suspect' (Achebe 1987: 99). These words of Ikem Osodi, Chinua Achebe's fictional martyr to democracy, aptly reflect the tenor of this essay.

For sub-Saharan Africa in the 1990s, the liberal-democratic, free-enterprise model appears both unavoidable and, despite its limitations, defensible. It is unavoidable owing to the disparity in power between its proponents, the international financial institutions backed by the industrial powers, and individual African governments. What is negotiable are the details of recovery programmes. Nevertheless, in the absence of an immediate radical alternative, the official model offers some benefits. It affords a scheme, albeit draconian, to stabilize external and fiscal accounts under harsh economic circumstances. It encourages governments to scale down their economic responsibilities to accord with their generally limited capacities. Shrinking the state may also redirect entrepreneurial energies into productive economic activities by lowering the premium attached to political power. Broadening the sphere and security of private initiative may discourage capital flight and attract sympathetic consideration of debt-relief. In the political realm, the new consensus focuses on the critical tasks of rebuilding the responsiveness, discipline, and capacities of governments. Democratization, limited and fragile though it will be, not only overturns despots, but also fosters more accountable governments. Freedoms of association, assembly, and expression provide some scope for organizational pluralism and the empowerment of the poor.

Yet 'all certitude must now be suspect'. Some have declared an end of history as liberal-democratic capitalism purportedly emerges victorious on a world scale (Fukuyama 1989). But announcements of the demise of radical alternatives are premature. Will the liberal-democratic, free-enterprise model prove equal to Africa's challenges in the twenty-first century – mass poverty, environmental degradation, and social conflict? The strategy is too top-down, imposed by governments beleaguered by domestic discontent and external pressure. Weakly grounded democratic structures buffeted by economic crisis and deep cleavages may not long endure. The ascendant ideology's stress on traditional exports and import liberalization aggravates Africa's structural dependency. Free-market remedies, especially with inadequate external assistance, are unlikely to reduce significantly absolute poverty, or the deforestation and soil erosion that such poverty entails.

Notions of people-centred development will therefore stay very much alive. This self-reliant, participatory, interventionist, and needs-oriented approach offers remedies to defects in the prevailing market-oriented model. Where it is weak is in the politics of its implementation. Whether this approach would need to take a socialist or capitalist coloration, or neither, remains to be seen. No end of ideology is in sight in sub-Saharan Africa.

NOTES

1 THE REDISCOVERY OF POLITICS

1 Structural adjustment was originally aimed at rectifying balance-of-payments deficits. This is still the goal of IMF adjustment programmes. But the World Bank now defines these programmes very broadly as policy reforms involving 'changes in relative prices and institutions designed to make the economy more efficient, more flexible, and better able to use resources and thereby to engineer sustainable long-term growth' (World Bank 1988a): 1.

2 Reported in Harsch 1988a: 57. For supporting assessments, see Ravenhill 1988: 179–210; and Mosley and Smith 1989: 321–55.

3 The Economic Commission for Africa and the South Commission (chaired by Julius Nyerere of Tanzania) attach much greater causal importance to external economic dependency. See UNECA 1989: 5; South Commission 1990: 53–73.

2 FALSE STARTS: CAPITALIST AND SOCIALIST

1 For more details, see Sandbrook with Barker 1985, chs. 3 and 4.

2 The following educational statistics are from World Bank 1988d.

3 Ironically, the ZANU government professes socialism. However, in practice, the multiracial business class has blunted the government's radicalism, a process dramatically illustrated by the promulgation in May 1989 of a favourable investment code and the president's decision in April 1990 not to proceed with a one-party state without obtaining the electorate's concurrence in a referendum. For a study which portrays African bourgeoisies as a relatively strong class, see Kennedy 1988.

4 'Political opponents show no mercy because struggles take place in a dual context of material scarcity and political insecurity. When the gross national product is low and the maintenance of a position of power depends solely upon the disposition of the Prince, the temptation is great to exploit one's position to the full. This explains the unbridled rapacity of political entrepreneurs and the violence that envelopes them.'

5 Nigerian commentators suspect that the current president, Lieutenant-General Ibrahim Babangida, is covertly attempting to entrench his personal rule in the transition process.

6 In 1985–7, Zambia undertook an IMF and World Bank-sponsored structural adjustment programme designed to move its highly regulated economy to market pricing and tight demand-management. In May 1987, Kaunda abandoned this programme to return to a heavy reliance on administrative controls, including price controls and administrative allocations of foreign exchange. The economy deteriorated further. Thus, the government again adopted a market-oriented approach in 1989, gaining the IMF's support in July 1990.

7 See the statistics recorded in World Bank 1983: 102, and World Bank 1988b: 115. On Tanzania, see Mukandala 1983: 254.

8 Computed from Sivard 1987, table on pp. 29–31.

3 CREATING AND ENABLING LIBERAL STATES

1 The equivalents in United States dollars are calculated at the unofficial rate of exchange. Although the official rate of exchange in both years was 2.75 cedis to the US dollar, unofficially the average rate of exchange moved from 7.02 cedis to 21.42 cedis to the US dollar. See World Bank, *World Tables*, 1988. Other conversions to US dollars are calculated on official rates, as they do not diverge significantly from unofficial rates.

2 However, some of Zimbabwe's parastatals have played an important economic role. For instance, Zimbabwe's marketing boards for tobacco and grain have facilitated exports by negotiating prices and guaranteeing the regularity of supply. (I'm indebted to Robin Cohen for this observation.)

3 Cf. Tanzi 1990.

4 DEMOCRATIZING LIBERAL STATES

1 However, in January 1991, Mugabe announced that he was abandoning for now his quest to make Zimbabwe a one-party state. This followed the rejection of this proposal by the Central Committee of the governing party.

2 But such tolerance is easily rescinded: the Babangida regime in Nigeria cracked down on journalists, among others, following the abortive coup attempt in April 1990; and the Kenyan government has harassed the editor of the respected and periodically banned *Nairobi Law Monthly*.

3 Zaire was only to receive economic assistance channelled through non-governmental organizations.

4 Quoted with permission of Fela Anikulapo-Kuti and Kalakuta Ltd., Lagos.

5 FROM RECOVERY TO TRANSFORMATION?

1 For a survey of the ideas of the African left in the mid-1980s, see Turok 1986: 56–71.

2 See especially, Amin 1976; Amin 1990.

3 A 'people's organization' is an association whose *raison d'être* is the promotion of its members' interests, whose internal procedures are democratic, and whose operation is not wholly dependent upon external funding or initiative. Examples are peasant associations, credit associations, cooperatives, independent trade unions, village improvement societies, and professional associations. 'Voluntary organizations', such as human-rights associations, development NGOs, and environmental groups, 'pursue a social mission driven by a commitment to shared values.' See Korten 1990: 2, 101–2.

REFERENCES

Abernethy, D. 1988. 'Bureaucratic Growth and Economic Stagnation in Sub-Saharan Africa'. In S. K. Commins, ed., *Africa's Development Challenges and the World Bank*. Boulder, CO: Lynne Rienner, pp. 179–214.

Achebe, C. 1987. *Anthills of the Savannah*. London: William Heinemann.

Adamolekun, L. 1989. 'Public Sector Management Improvement in Sub-Saharan Africa: the World Bank Experience'. In M. J. Balogun and G. Mutahaba, eds., *Economic Restructuring and African Public Administration*. West Hartford: Kumarian Press, pp. 67–90.

Adedeji, A. 1990. 'Putting the People First'. Opening Address, International Conference on Popular Participation in the Recovery Process in Africa, Arusha, Tanzania, Feb. 12.

Africa Research Bulletin. 1989–91. Various issues.

African Spectrum (Lagos).

Ake, C. 1987. 'The African Context of Human Rights', *Africa Today*, vol. 34, no. 1/2, pp. 5–12.

1990. 'Democracy and Development', *West Africa*, Mar. 26, p. 591.

Akinola, A. A. 1989. 'A Critique of Nigeria's Proposed Two-Party System', *Journal of Modern African Studies*, vol. 27, no. 1, pp. 109–23.

Amin, S. 1976. *Unequal Development: An Essay on the Social Formations of Peripheral Capitalism*. New York: Monthly Review Press.

1987. 'Democracy and National Strategy in the Periphery', *Third World Quarterly*, vol. 9, no. 4, pp. 1129–56.

1990. *Maldevelopment: Anatomy of a Global Failure*. London: Zed Books.

Anderson, D. 1989. 'Infrastructure Pricing Policies and the Public Revenue in African Countries', *World Development*, vol. 17, no. 4, pp. 525–42.

Ankomah, B. 1986. 'Ghana: Where Truth is on Holiday', *Index on Censorship*, vol. 15, no. 4, pp. 33–4.

Anon. 1988. 'Struggle for Dignity', *West Africa*, November 21–7, pp. 2176–7.

Ayisi, R. A. 1991. 'Mozambique: Back to the Stone Age', *Africa Report*, vol. 36, no. 1, pp. 37–9.

Baran, P. 1957. *The Political Economy of Growth*. New York: Monthly Review Press.

Bardhan, P. 1984. *The Political Economy of Development in India*. Oxford: Basil Blackwell.

Barros, R. 1986. 'The Left and Democracy: Recent Debates in Latin America', *Telos*, no. 68, pp. 49–70.

Bayart, J.-F. 1989. *L'État en Afrique: La politique du ventre*. Paris: Editions Fayard.

Bendix, R. 1962. *Max Weber: An Intellectual Portrait*. Garden City: Doubleday.

Bhagwati, J. 1966. *The Economics of Underdeveloped Countries*. New York: McGraw-Hill.

Bjorkman, I. 1989. *'Mother, Sing for Me': People's Theatre in Kenya*. London: Zed Books.

Bourke, G. 1991. 'Côte d'Ivoire: A New Broom?' *Africa Report*, vol. 36, no. 1, pp. 13–16.

Brown, J. M. 1985. *Modern India: The Origins of an Asian Democracy*. New Delhi: Oxford University Press.

Browne, R. S. 1989. 'Africa: Time for a New Development Strategy'. In M. Martin and T. Randal, eds., *Development and Change in the Modern World*. New York: Oxford University Press, pp. 399–408.

Bryce, J. 1989. 'Fela Anikulapo-Kuti: "Animal Can't Dash me Human Rights"', *Index on Censorship*, vol. 19, no. 9, pp. 12–13.

Callaghy, T. M. 1989. 'Toward State Capability and Embedded Liberalism in the Third World: Lessons for Adjustment', in J. Nelson, ed., *Fragile Coalitions: The Politics of Economic Adjustment*. New Brunswick, NJ: Transaction Books, pp. 115–38.

   1990. 'Lost between State and Market: The Politics of Economic Adjustment in Ghana, Zambia and Nigeria', in J. Nelson, ed., *Economic Crisis and Policy Choice: The Politics of Adjustment in the Third World*. Princeton: Princeton University Press, pp. 257–320.

Cardoso, F. H. 1986. 'Entrepreneurs and the Transition Process: The Brazilian Case'. In G. O'Donnell et al., eds., *Transitions from Authoritarian Rule: Comparative Perspectives*, Baltimore: Johns Hopkins University Press, pp. 137–53.

   1987. 'Democracy in Latin America', *Politics and Society*, vol. 16, pp. 23–41.

Chazan, N. 1982. 'The New Politics of Participation in Tropical Africa', *Comparative Politics*, vol. 14, pp. 169–89.

Clapham, C. 1989. 'The State and Revolution in Ethiopia', *Review of African Political Economy*, no. 44, pp. 5–17.

Clark, J. 1991. *Democratizing Development: The Role of Voluntary Organizations*. West Hartford: Kumarian Press.

Clark, J. with C. Allison 1989. *Zambia: Debt and Poverty*. Oxford: Oxfam.

Colclough, C. 1985. 'Competing Paradigms in the Debate about Agricultural Pricing Policy', *International Development Studies Bulletin*, vol. 16, no. 3, pp. 39–46.

Collier, D. (ed.) 1979. *The New Authoritarianism in Latin America*. Princeton: Princeton University Press.

Cook, P. and C. Kirkpatrick 1988. 'Privatisation in Less Developed Countries: An Overview'. In Cook and Kirkpatrick, eds., *Privatisation in Less Developed Countries*. New York: St Martin's Press, pp. 3–44.

Corkery, F. and J. Bossuyt (eds.) 1990. *Governance and Institutional Development in Sub-Saharan Africa: Summary Report of a Seminar of 28–30 March 1990*. Maastricht: European Centre for Development and Public Management.

Coulon, C. 1988. 'Senegal: The Development and Fragility of Semidemocracy'. In L. Diamond et al., eds., *Democracy in Developing Countries: Africa*, Boulder, CO: Lynne Rienner, pp. 141–78.

Crook, R. E. 1988. 'State Capacity and Economic Development: The Case of Côte d'Ivoire', *International Development Studies Bulletin*, vol. 19, no. 4, pp. 19–25.

   1990. 'State, Society and Political Institutions in Côte d'Ivoire and Ghana', *Institute of Development Studies Bulletin*, vol. 21, no. 4, pp. 24–34.

Cunningham, F. 1987. *Democratic Theory and Socialism*. Cambridge: Cambridge University Press.

Dag Hammarskjold Foundation 1975. *What Now: Another Development*. Uppsala: Dag Hammarskjold Foundation.

Decalo, S. 1989. *Psychoses of Power: African Personal Dictatorships*. Boulder, CO: Westview.

Diamond, L. 1988a. *Class, Ethnicity and Democracy in Nigeria: The Failure of the First Republic*. London: Macmillan.

   1988b. 'Nigeria: Pluralism, Statism and the Struggle for Democracy'. In L. Diamond et al., eds., *Democracy in Developing Countries: Africa*, Boulder, CO: Lynne Rienner, pp. 33–92.

   1988c. 'Introduction: Roots of Failure, Seeds of Hope'. In L. Diamond, J. J. Linz, and S. M. Lipset, eds., *Democracy in Developing Countries: Africa*, Boulder, CO: Lynne Rienner, pp. 1–32.

Diop, M. C. and M. Diouf 1990. *Le Sénégal sous Abdou Diouf*. Paris: Karthala.

Dobell, J. P. 1978. 'The Corruption of a State', *American Political Science Review*, vol. 72, no. 3, pp. 958–73.

Douglas, W. A. 1972. *Developing Democracy*. Washington, DC: Heldref.

Dumont, R. 1966. *False Start in Africa*. London: Sphere Books. (Published in French in 1962.)

Egero, B. 1987. *Mozambique, A Dream Undone: The Political Economy of Democracy, 1974–85*. Uppsala: Nordic African Institute.

Elliott, C. 1988. 'Structural Adjustment in the Longer Run: Some Uncomfortable Questions'. In S. K. Commins, ed., *Africa's Development challenges and the World Bank*, Boulder, CO: Lynne Rienner, pp. 159–78.

Evans, P. 1989. 'Predatory, Developmental and Other Apparatuses: A Comparative Political Economy Perspective on the Third World State', *Sociological Forum*, vol. 4, no. 4, pp. 561–87.

Fatton, R. 1987. *The Making of a Liberal democracy: Senegal's Passive Revolution*. Boulder, CO: Lynne Rienner.

Friedman, M. 1962. *Capitalism and Freedom*. Chicago: University of Chicago Press.

Fukuyama, F. 1989. 'The End of History?' *The National Interest*, vol. 16, pp. 3–18.

Gerschenkron, A. 1963. *Economic Backwardness in Historical Perspective*. Cambridge, MA: Harvard University Press.

Gerster, R. 1989. 'How to Ruin a Country: The Case of Togo', *IFDA Dossier*, no. 71, May/June, pp. 25–36.

Good, K. 1989. 'Debt and the One-Party State in Zambia', *Journal of Modern African Studies*, vol. 27, no. 2, pp. 297–313.

Gow, D. and J. VanSant 1983. 'Beyond the Rhetoric of Rural Development Participation: How Can it be Done?' *World Development*, vol. 11, no. 5, pp. 427–45.

Grant, J. 1981. *The State of the World's Children 1980–81*. New York: UNICEF.

Green, R. H. 1987. 'Killing the Dream: The Political and Human Economy of War in Sub-Saharan Africa', Brighton, Sussex: Institute of Development Studies, Discussion Paper no. 238.

Harsch, E. 1988a. 'Recovery or Relapse?' *Africa Report*, vol. 33, no. 6, pp. 56–9.

    1988b. 'Burkina Faso: A Revolution Derailed', *Africa Report*, vol. 33, no. 2, pp. 33–9.

    1989. 'Ghana: On the Road to Recovery', *Africa Report*, vol. 34, no. 4, pp. 21–6.

Hartlyn, J. and S. A. Morley. 1986. 'Bureaucratic-Authoritarian Regimes in Comparative Perspective', in J. Hartlyn and S. A. Morley, eds.,

Latin American Political Economy, Boulder, CO: Westview, pp. 38–53.

Hayward, F. M. and S. N. Grovogui. 1986. 'Persistence and Change in Senegalese Electoral Processes', in F. M. Hayward, ed., *Elections in Independent Africa*, Boulder, CO: Westview, pp. 239–70.

Hecht, R. 1983. 'The Ivory Coast "Miracle": What Benefits for Peasant Farmers?' *Journal of Modern African Studies*, vol. 21, no. 1, pp. 25–53.

Helleiner, G. K. 1990. 'Structural Adjustment and Long-Term Development in Sub-Saharan Africa', Centro Studi Luca d'Agliano (Torino, Italy) and Queen Elizabeth House Development Studies (Cambridge) Working Paper no. 18.

Herbst, J. 1989. 'Political Impediments to Economic Rationality: Explaining Zimbabwe's Failure to Reform its Public Sector', *Journal of Modern African Studies*, vol. 27, no. 1, pp. 67–84.

1990. 'The Structural Adjustment of Politics in Africa', *World Development*, vol. 18, no. 7, pp. 949–58.

Hermele, K. 1990. *Mozambique Crossroads: Economy and Politics in the Era of Structural Adjustment*. Bergen: Chr. Michelsen Institute.

Hicks, N. 1991. 'Expenditure Reductions in Developing Countries Revisited', *Journal of International Development*, vol. 3, no. 1, pp. 29–38.

Holm, J. 1982. 'Liberal democracy and Rural Development in Botswana', *African Studies Review*, vol. 25, no. 1, pp. 83–102.

1988. 'Botswana: A Paternalistic Democracy', in L. Diamond et al., eds., *Democracy in Developing Countries: Africa*, Boulder, CO: Lynne Rienner, pp. 179–216.

Horvat, B. 1982. *The Political Economy of Socialism: A Marxist Social Theory*. Armonk, NY: Sharpe.

Hughes, A. 1982–83. 'The Limits of "Consociational Democracy" in the Gambia', *Civilisations*, vol. 32/33, no. 1/2, pp. 65–96.

Hunt, A. 1980. 'Taking Democracy Seriously', in A. Hunt, ed., *Marxism and Democracy*, London: Lawrence and Wishart, pp. 7–20.

Hutchful, E. 1986. 'New Elements in Militarism: Ethiopia, Ghana and Burkina', *International Journal*, vol. 41, no. 4, pp. 802–30.

International Labour Organization 1976. *Employment, Growth and Basic Needs: A One-World Problem*. Geneva: ILO.

IMF [International Monetary Fund] Survey, various issues.

Jerve, A. M. and J. Naustdalslid 1990. *Research on Local Government in Tanzania*. Bergen: Chr. Michelsen Institute, no. D1990:5.

Johnson, C. 1987. 'Political Institutions and Economic Performance: The Government-Business Relationship in Japan, South Korea, and Taiwan', in F. C. Deyo, ed., *The Political Economy of the New Asian Industrialism*, Ithaca, NY: Cornell University Press, pp. 135–64.

Joseph, R. 1987. *Democracy and Prebendal Politics in Nigeria: The Rise and Fall of the Second Republic*. Cambridge: Cambridge University Press.

Kapuscinski, R. 1983. *The Emperor: Downfall of an Autocrat*. London: Quartet.

Keane, J. 1988. *Democracy and Civil Society*. London: Verso.

Kennedy, P. 1988 *African Capitalism*. Cambridge: Cambridge University Press.

Khalilzedeh-Shirazi, R. and A. Shah 1991. 'Tax Reform in Developing Countries', *Finance and Development*, vol. 28, no. 2, pp. 44–6.

Killick, T. 1989. *A Reaction Too Far: Economic Theory and the Role of the State in Developing Countries*. London: Overseas Development Institute.

Kitching, G. 1980. *Class and Economic Change in Kenya: The Making of an African Petite-Bourgeoisie*. New Haven: Yale University Press.

Ki-Zerbo, J. 1986. 'Africa – Silent Continent?' *Index on Censorship*, no. 2, pp. 16–18.

Kohli, A. 1986. 'Development and Democracy', in J. P. Lewis and V. Kallab, eds., *Development Strategies Reconsidered*, New Brunswick, NJ: Transaction Books, pp. 153–83.

1989. *The State and Poverty in India: The Politics of Reform*. Cambridge: Cambridge University Press.

Korten, D. C. 1990. *Getting to the 21st Century: Voluntary Action and the Global Agenda*. West Hartford: Kumarian Press.

Lemarchand, R. 1988. 'The State, the Parallel Economy, and the Changing Structure of Patronage Systems', in D. Rothchild and N. Chazan, eds., *The Precarious Balance: State and Society in Africa*, Boulder, CO: Westview, pp. 67–99.

Leslie, W. J. 1987. *The World Bank and Structural Transformation in Developing Countries: The Case of Zaire*. Boulder, CO: Lynne Rienner.

Liniger-Goumaz, M. 1988. *Small is Not Beautiful: The Story of Equatorial Guinea*. London: C. Hurst.

Lonsdale, J. 1989. 'African Pasts in Africa's Future', *Canadian Journal of African Studies*, vol. 23, no. 1, pp. 126–46.

Loxley, J. 1991. 'The Political Economy of Economic Reform in Sub-Saharan Africa: The Case of Ghana', Paper presented to the Development Studies Seminar, University of Toronto, Feb. 8.

Luke, D. F. 1989. 'The Politics of Economic Decline in Sierra Leone', *Journal of Modern African Studies*, vol. 27, no. 1, pp. 133–41.

Mamdani, M. 1988. 'Uganda in Transition: Two Years of the NRA/NRM', *Third World Quarterly*, vol. 10, no. 3, pp. 1155–81.

Mannick, A. R. 1979. *Mauritius: The Development of a Plural Society*. Nottingham, UK: Spokesman.

Marcussen, H. S. and J. E. Torp 1982. *Internationalization of Capital: Prospects for the Third World*. London: Zed Press.

Martin, G. 1986. 'Ideologie et praxis dans la Révolution Populaire du 4 Aôut 1983 au Burkina Faso', *Genève-Afrique*, vol. 24, no. 1, pp. 35–62.

1989. 'Revolutionary Democracy, Socio-Political conflict and Militarization in Burkina Faso, 1983–88', in P. Meyns and D. Nabudere, eds., *Democracy and the One-Party State in Africa*. Hamburg: Institut fur Afrika-Kunde.

Mawhood, P. 1987. 'Decentralization and the Third World in the 1980s', *Planning and Administration*, vol. 16, no. 1, pp. 10–22.

Mbanefo, A. C. I. 1975. 'The Management of Public Enterprises Control and Autonomy – External and Internal Problems', in A. H. Rweyamamu and G. Hyden, eds., *A Decade of Public Administration in Africa*, Nairobi: East Africa Literature Bureau, pp. 289–99.

McGowan, P. and T. Johnson, 1986. 'Sixty Coups in Thirty Years: Further Evidence regarding African Coups', *Journal of Modern African Studies*, vol. 24, pp. 539–46.

McNamara, R. S. 1985. *The Challenges for Sub-Saharan Africa*. Washington, D.C.: Sir John Crawford Memorial Lecture.

Midgley, J. *et al.* 1986. *Community Participation, Social Development and the State*. London: Metheun.

Miles, W. 1987. *Elections in Nigeria: A Grassroots Perspective*. Boulder, CO: Lynne Rienner.

Miller, D. 1989. *Market, State and Community: Theoretical Foundations of Market Socialism*. London: Oxford University Press.

Moharir, V. V. 1990. 'Capacity Building Initiative for Sub-Saharan Africa', in *Sub-Saharan Africa: Beyond Adjustment: A Seminar Report*, Maastricht: Ministry of Foreign Affairs, Netherlands, pp. 104–14.

Moore, B. 1966. *Social Origins of Dictatorship and Democracy*. Boston: Beacon Press.

Morna, C. L. 1988. 'Ghana: The Privatization Drive', *Africa Report*, vol. 33, no. 6, pp. 60–2.

1989. 'Surviving Structural Adjustment', *Africa Report*, vol. 34, no. 5, pp. 45–8.

1990. 'World Bank: A New Development Compact?' *Africa Report*, vol. 35, no. 1, pp. 50–3.

1991. 'Enticing Investment', *Africa Report*, vol. 36, no. 1, pp. 40–3.

Mosley, P. and L. Smith. 1989. 'Structural Adjustment and Agricultural Performance in Sub-Saharan Africa, 1980–1987', *Journal of International Development*, vol. 1, no. 3, pp. 321–55.

Mukandala, R. 1983. 'Trends in Civil Service Size and Income in Tanzania', *Canadian Journal of African Studies*, vol. 17, pp. 253–63.

Munishi, G. K. 1989. 'Bureaucratic Feudalism, Accountability and Development in the Third World: The Case of Tanzania', in J. G. Jabbra and O. P. Dwivedi, eds. *Public Service Accountability*, West Hartford: Kumarian Press, pp. 153–67.

Murumba, C. K. 1987. 'Sharing Responsibility and Resources for Effective Central-Local Relationships in Kenya', *Planning and Administration*, vol. 14, no. 1, pp. 100–9.

Nellis, J. R. 1972. *Who Pays Tax in Kenya?* Uppsala: Scandinavian Institute of African Studies, Research Report no. 11.

  1986. 'Public Enterprises in Sub-Saharan African', *World Bank Discussion Paper*, no. 1. Washington, DC: World Bank, November.

Nellis, J. R. and S. Kikeri 1989. 'Public Enterprise Reform: Privatization and the World Bank', *World Development*, vol. 27, no. 5, pp. 659–72.

Nolutshungu, S. C. 1990. 'Fragments of a Democracy: Reflections on Class and Politics in Nigeria', *Third World Quarterly*, vol. 12, no. 1.

Nove, A. 1983. *The Economics of Feasible Socialism*. London: Allen and Unwin.

Nowak, M. and T. Swinehart. 1989. 'Botswana', *Human rights in Developing Countries: 1989 Yearbook*, Kehl, Germany: N. P. Engel Publisher, pp. 146–7.

Nursey-Bray, P. 1983. 'Consensus and Community: The Theory of African One-Party Democracy', in G. Duncan, ed., *Democratic Theory and Practice*, Cambridge: Cambridge University Press, pp. 96–111.

Nyong'o, P. A. ed. 1987. *Popular Struggles for Democracy in Africa*. London: Zed Press.

Ogbonna, M. N. 1975. 'Tax Evasion in Nigeria', *Africa Today*, vol. 22, pp. 53–61.

Onimode, B. 1988. *A Political Economy of the African Crisis*. London: Zed Books.

Osaghae, E. 1989. 'The Strengthening of Local Government and the Operation of Federalism in Nigeria', *Journal of Commonwealth and Comparative Politics*, vol. 27, no. 3, pp. 347–63.

Ottaway, M. 1987. 'The Crisis of the Socialist State in Africa', in Z. Ergas, ed., *The African State in Transition*, London: Macmillan, pp. 169–90.

  1988. 'Mozambique: From Symbolic Socialism to Symbolic Reform', *Journal of Modern African Studies*, vol. 26, no. 2, pp. 211–26.

Parson, J. 1984. *Botswana: Liberal Democracy and the Labor Reserve in Southern Africa*. Boulder, CO: Westview.

Pateman, R. 1990. 'Liberté, Egalité, Fraternité: Aspects of the Eritrean Revolution', *Journal of Modern African Studies*, vol. 28, no. 3, pp. 457–72.

p'Bitek, O. 1971. *Two Songs*. Nairobi: East African Publishing House.

Peeler, J. 1985. *Latin American Democracies*. Chapel Hill, NC: University of North Carolina Press.

Picard, L. A. 1987. *The Politics of Development in Botswana: A Model for Success?* Boulder, CO: Lynne Rienner.

Picard, L. A. and N. L. Graybeal. 1988. 'Structural Adjustment, Public Sector Reform and the West African Political System', Paper presented to the African Studies Association Conference, Chicago, Oct. 26–30.

Polanyi, K. 1944. *The Great Transformation: The Political and Economic Origins of Our Times*. Boston: Beacon Press.

Rao, V. 1984–85. 'Democracy and Economic Development', *Studies in Comparative International Development*, vol. 19, pp. 64–85.

Ravenhill, J. 1988. 'Adjustment with Growth: A Fragile Consensus', *Journal of Modern African Studies*, vol. 26, no. 2, pp. 179–210.

 1990. 'Reversing Africa's Economic Decline: No Easy Answers', *World Policy Journal*, vol. 7, no. 4, pp. 703–32.

Rondinelli, D. A. *et al.* 1984. *Decentralization in Developing Countries: A Review of Recent Experience*. World Bank, Staff Working Paper no. 581.

Rothchild, D. and M. Foley 1987. 'Ideology and Policy in Afro-Marxist Regimes', in E. Keller and D. Rothchild, eds., *Afro-Marxist Regimes: Ideology and Public Policy*, Boulder, CO: Lynne Rienner, pp. 281–321.

Rothchild, D. and E. Gyimah-Boadi 1989. 'Populism in Ghana and Burkina Faso', *Current History*, vol. 88, no. 538, pp. 221–4.

Salole, G. 1991. 'Not Seeing the Wood for the Trees: Searching for Indigenous NGOs in the Forest of Voluntary Self-Help Associations', *Journal of Social Development in Africa*, vol. 6, no. 1, pp. 5–17.

Samoff, J. 1989. 'Popular Initiatives and Local Government in Tanzania', *Journal of Developing Areas*, vol. 24, no. 1, pp. 1–18.

Sandbrook, R. 1982. *The Politics of Basic Needs: Assaulting Urban Poverty in Africa*. London: Heinemann.

 1988. 'Liberal Democracy in Africa: A Socialist-Revisionist Perspective', *Canadian Journal of African Studies*, vol. 22, pp. 240–67.

 1991. 'Economic Crisis, Structural Adjustment and the State in Sub-Saharan Africa', in Dharam Ghai, ed., *The IMF and the South: The Social Impact of Crisis and Adjustment*, London: Zed Books, pp. 95–114.

Sandbrook, R. with J. Barker. 1985. *The Politics of Africa's Economic Stagnation*, Cambridge: Cambridge University Press.

Schatz, S. 1984. 'Pirate Capitalism and the Inert Economy of Nigeria', *Journal of Modern African Studies*, vol. 22, no. 1, pp. 45–57.

Schatzberg, M. 1988. *The Dialectics of Oppression in Zaire*. Bloomington: Indiana University Press.

Schissel, H. 1989. 'Africa's Underground Economy', *Africa Report*, vol. 34, no. 1, pp. 43–6.

Shalizi, Z. and L. Squire 1988. *Tax Policy in Sub-Saharan Africa: A Framework for Analysis*. World Bank, Policy and Research Series no. 2.

Shields, T. 1990. 'Kenya: Lawyers vs. the Law', *Africa Report*, vol. 35, no. 4, pp. 13–16.

Shivji, I. 1988. *Fight My Beloved Continent: New Democracy in Africa*. Harare, Zimbabwe: SAPES Trust.

1991. 'The Democracy Debate in Africa: Tanzania', *Review of African Political Economy*, no. 50, pp. 79–91.

Simiyu, V. G. 1987. 'The Democratic Myth in African Traditional Societies', in W. O. Oyugi and A. Gitonga, eds. *Democratic Theory and Practice in Africa*, Nairobi: Heinemann, pp. 49–70.

Sivard, R. L. 1987. *World Military and Social Expenditures, 1986–7*. Washington, DC: World Priorities Inc.

Somerville, C. M. 1988. 'Economic Crisis, Economic Reform, and Political Democracy: The Case of Senegal', Paper presented to the Annual Meeting of the African Studies Association, Chicago, 28–31 Oct.

South Commission. 1990. *The Challenge to the South: Report of the South Commission*. London: Oxford University Press.

Spear, T. 1989. 'Tanzania: Return to the Land', *Africa Report*, vol. 34, no. 2, pp. 45–7.

Szeftel, M. 1982. 'Political Graft and the Spoils System in Zambia', *Review of African Political Economy*, no. 24, pp. 4–21.

Tanzi, V. 1990. 'Fiscal Issues in Adjustment Programs in Developing Countries', Torino, Centro Studi Luca d'Agliano, Working paper no. 26, September.

Therborn, G. 1979. 'The Travail of Latin American Democracy', *New Left Review*, no. 113/114, pp. 71–109.

Topouzis, D. 1989. 'Guinea: Conté's Challenge', *Africa Report*, vol. 34, no. 6, pp. 38–41.

1990. 'Wangari Maathai: Empowering the Grassroots', *Africa Report*, vol. 35, no. 5, pp. 31–2.

Tordoff, W. 1988. 'Local Administration in Botswana', *Public Administration and Development*, vol. 8, no. 2, pp. 183–202.

Turok, B. 1986. 'The Left in Africa Today', in B. Munslow, ed., *Africa: Problems in the Transition to Socialism*, London: Zed Press, pp. 56–71.

Umbadda, S. 1989. 'Economic Crisis in the Sudan: Impact and Responses', Paper Delivered at the Conference on Economic Crisis and Third World Countries, Kingston, Jamaica, 3–6 April.

United Nations 1991. *Economic Crisis in Africa*, Report of the Secretary General. New York: United Nations.

United Nations Development Programme. 1990. *Human Development Report 1990*. New York: Oxford University Press.

United Nations, Economic Commission for Africa. 1989. *African Alternative Framework to Structural Adjustment Programmes for Socio-Economic Recovery and Transformation*. Addis Ababa: Economic Commission for Africa.

  1990. *African Charter for Popular Participation in Development and Transformation (Arusha 1990)*. Addis Ababa: ECA.

Van de Walle, N. 1989. 'Privatization in Developing Countries: A Review of the Issues', *World Development*, vol. 17, no. 5, pp. 601–15.

Volman, D. 1987. 'U.S. Policy in Africa: Walk Covertly and Carry a Stinger', *New African*, no. 234, pp. 14–16.

Weber, M. 1947. *The Theory of Social and Economic Organization*. New York: The Free Press.

Weekly Review (Nairobi).

Weinstein, W. 1983. 'Human Rights and Development in Africa: Dilemmas and Options', *Daedalus*, no. 112, pp. 171–96.

Wekwete, K. 1988. 'The Local Government System in Zimbabwe', *Planning and Administration*, vol. 15, no. 1, pp. 18–27.

West Africa. Various dates, 1989–91.

White, G. 1984. 'Developmental States and Socialist Industrialization in the Third World', *Journal of Development Studies*, vol. 21, no. 1, pp. 97–120.

Whiteman, K. 1988. 'Mitterand Mark 2: The End of an Era?' *Africa Report*, vol. 33, no. 5, pp. 50–4.

  1991. 'France/Africa: The Gallic Paradox', *Africa Report*, vol. 36, no. 1, pp. 17–20.

Wilcox, D. L. 1982. 'Black African States', in J. L. Curry and J. R. Dassin, eds., *Press Control around the World*, New York: Praeger, pp. 209–32.

Willame, J.-C. 1988. 'Political Succession in Zaire, or Back to Machiavelli', *Journal of Modern African Studies*, vol. 26, no. 1, pp. 37–49.

Wils, F. 1988. 'Participation and Development: Old and Newer Relationships', *Planning and Administration*, vol. 15, no. 1, pp. 73–7.

Wisner, B. 1988. *Power and Needs in Africa: Basic Human Needs and Development Policies*. London: Earthscan.

Wood, R. E. 1986. *From Marshall Plan to Debt Crisis: Foreign Aid and Development Choices in the World Economy*. Los Angeles: University of California Press.

Woodward, P. 1987. 'Is the Sudan Governable?' *British Society for Middle Eastern Studies Bulletin*, vol. 13, no. 2, pp. 137–49.

World Bank 1981. *Accelerated Development in Sub-Saharan Africa: An Agenda for Action*. Washington, DC: World Bank.

   1983. *World Development Report 1983*. New York: Oxford University Press.

   1988a. *Adjustment Lending: An Evaluation of Ten Years of Experience*. Washington, DC: World Bank.

   1988b. *World Development Report 1988*. New York: Oxford University Press.

   1988c. *Social Indicators of Development 1988*. Washington, DC: World Bank.

   1988d. *Education in Sub-Saharan Africa: Policies for Adjustment, Revitalization and Expansion*. Washington, DC: World Bank.

   1989a. *Sub-Saharan Africa: From Crisis to Sustainable Growth*. Washington, DC: World Bank.

   1989b. *Africa's Adjustment and Growth in the 1980s*. Washington, DC: World Bank.

   1990a. *World Development Report 1990*. New York: Oxford University Press.

   1990b. *A Framework for Capacity Building in Policy Analysis and Economic Management in Sub-Saharan Africa*. Washington, DC: World Bank.

   1990c. *World Debt Tables 1990–91*. Washington, DC: World Bank.

   1991a. *World Development Report 1991*. New York: Oxford University Press.

   1991b. *The Reform of Public Sector Management: Lessons from Experience*. Washington, DC: Policy and Research Series 18, World Bank.

Wuyts, M. 1989. 'Economic Management and Adjustment Policies in Mozambique', Paper Delivered at the Conference on Economic Crisis and Third World Countries, Kingston, Jamaica, 3–6 April.

Young, C. and T. Turner 1986. *The Rise and Decline of the Zairean State*. Madison: University of Wisconsin Press.

Zack-Williams, A. B. 1990. 'Sierra Leone: Crisis and Despair', *Review of African Political Economy*, no. 49, pp. 22–33.

   1991. 'Crisis, Structural Adjustment, and Creative Survival in Sierra Leone', Paper presented to the Annual Conference of the Canadian Association of African Studies, York University, Toronto, May.

INDEX

Operation Manta, 100
Organization of African Unity (OAU), 19,
136, 138, 143

parallel economy, *see* informal economy
participation
in communities, 18, 74, 145
and development, 19, 138, 145
and socialism, 122–5
patrimonialism, 27–8; *see also*
neopatrimonialism
p'Bitek, Okot, 114
peasants, 27, 28, 36, 98, 123–4, 130–2
people-centred development, 19, 134–50
people's organizations, 109, 135, 141, 146,
147
defined, 153n
personal rule, *see* neopatrimonialism
'pirate capitalism', 30
political capacity, 24, 50–4, 85–6
political culture, 91–5
political leadership and democracy, 104–6
political parties and democracy, 90, 92,
96–8, 107, 147
political violence, 50–4
politics and economic growth, *see*
development ideology; states
popular culture and protest, 112–15
popular-nationalist approach, 126–32, 148
popular theatre, 112–13
population increase, 15, 16
poverty
and democracy, 118–20
dimensions, 5–9, 25, 122, 139
and markets, 4
and state-formation, 24
prebendalism, 28–9
precolonial polities, 92–4
Preferential Trade Area (PTA), 142
press freedom, 18, 91, 107–9, 152n
privatization, 18, 38, 63–70, 76–7
proletariat, 22, 26–7, 98
protectionism, in the North, 20
Provisional National Defence Council
(Ghana), 127–9
public enterprises, 22, 63–70; *see also*
marketing boards

Ratsiraka, Didier, 88
Rawlings, Flight-Lieutenant J.J., 10, 69,
108, 127–9
Reagan, Ronald, 118
Renamo (Mozambique), 36–8
Resistance Councils (Uganda), 90
retrenchment of public employees, 59–63,
76
'rumour-mongering', 114

Russia, 19, 37, 57, 99, 102, 123
Rwanda, 24

Sankara, Captain Thomas, 127, 129–32
São Tomé and Principe, 32, 89
Senegal
communalism, 97
democracy, 89–90, 94–5, 105–6, 110
economy, 6
and neopatrimonialism, 118
and poverty, 119
Senghor, Léopold, 92, 105–6, 110, 112
Shagari, Shehu, 111
Shivji, Issa, 126–7
Sierra Leone, 6–8, 31, 61, 71, 79
small industry, promotion of, 66
socialism, 4, 19, 23, 27
African cases, 34–9, 122–4
appeal of, 121–4
approaches to, 92, 125–34, 148
practical failings of, 121, 125, 126
social movements, 106, 110–11, 135, 144,
146; *see also* civil associations
South Africa, 102, 143
South Commission, 151n
Southern African Development
Coordination Conference (SADCC),
142, 143
Soviet Union, *see* Russia
Spain, 102
states
autonomy and political will, 22–3, 27,
54, 117, 137, 141
capacities of, 22–5 *passim*, 35, 39–55, 59,
77–86
centrality to growth prospects, 2–3, 14,
16–18, 39, 54–5, 77–8
interventionist strategies, 22, 56–9, 137,
143–4
liberal reform of, 17–20, 59–83
see also authoritarianism; democracy;
neopatrimonialism
structural adjustment programmes, 8
African cases, 10–11, 12, 34, 37–8, 128–9,
152n
and democracy, 98, 99
efficacy of, 10–11, 136
and political conditionality, 1–4 *passim*,
77–8, 100, 102–4
ingredients of, 9–10, 59–85, 134, 151n
sub-proletariat, 98
Sudan, 30, 96, 110
Swaziland, 24

Tanzania
economy, 6, 9
local government, 71, 73–4